Life is a Jukebox

Real Stories of Triumphs and Tragedies

By Rick Minerd

Order this book online at www.trafford.com
or email orders@trafford.com

Most Trafford titles are also available at major online book retailers.

Note for Librarians: A cataloguing record for this book is available from Library and Archives Canada at www.collectionscanada.ca/amicus/index-e.html

Printed in Victoria, BC, Canada.

ISBN: 978-1-4269-1326-6 (soft)
ISBN: 978-1-4269-1325-9 (hard)

Library of Congress Control Number: 2009931996

We at Trafford believe that it is the responsibility of us all, as both individuals and corporations, to make choices that are environmentally and socially sound. You, in turn, are supporting this responsible conduct each time you purchase a Trafford book, or make use of our publishing services. To find out how you are helping, please visit www.trafford.com/responsiblepublishing.html

Our mission is to efficiently provide the world's finest, most comprehensive book publishing service, enabling every author to experience success. To find out how to publish your book, your way, and have it available worldwide, visit us online at www.trafford.com

Trafford rev. 8/14/2009

 www.trafford.com

North America & international
toll-free: 1 888 232 4444 (USA & Canada)
phone: 250 383 6864 ♦ fax: 250 383 6804 ♦ email: info@trafford.com

The United Kingdom & Europe
phone: +44 (0)1865 487 395 ♦ local rate: 0845 230 9601
facsimile: +44 (0)1865 481 507 ♦ email: info.uk@trafford.com

I Talked My Way Through It

The following collection of short stories is like a manifest of names, as well as descriptions of people and experiences, and how their paths crossed mine. Some famous, some not so much but leaving indelible marks worth talking about.

I hope that through it I can explain whom, or as some may argue what I have become. Whether I am a who or a does not matter to me because getting to where ever it is I am has been interesting. Besides, all of us are both anyway.

The content of the stories I write comes from years of making my way through life by running my mouth. Sort of.

As a child I did that enough times to get what I wanted, and in many cases, what I did not. Nevertheless, I always got something. For instance, when I was in the fifth grade at Siebert Elementary School, the patrol boy unit that I was a member of was planning its annual picnic during the final week of school and I was making remarks to some kids who were not patrol boys about how awful for them it would be the next day to be sitting in a hot classroom all day while myself and the other patrol boys would be at the park, enjoying refreshments and playing ball.

Our teacher, Mrs. Bickle overheard the taunts and sent the rest of the class outside for extended recess and took me into what was called a cloakroom, also the area normally used when a student needed paddled. I expected the worst.

There I was verbally thrashed and my picnic privileges for the following day were revoked. An example of getting something I did not want. However, I talked my way out of being paddled, another example of the same thing and just one example of many more I will talk about later.

On the other hand, I would say that my triumphs are greater than my defeats; I have managed to talk my way into and around some pretty cool places and thus have met some rather impressive people.

I can write similar scenarios all day, whether I am tracking personal relationships, jobs I have held or friends and enemies that I have collected through the years. It is all about talking ones way through it.

As a radio announcer I was paid a little bit of money to talk on the air, and sometimes in a public forum such as emceeing a concert, hosting a school dance, a remote broadcast or anywhere the radio station was directing its listeners to go.

Being a radio personality my mouth may have opened more doors than I probably wanted, and probably several I should have left closed. Doors to new relationships for instance, including a few that lasted more than a morning, even a couple that could linger through an entire day and one or two that went way beyond a week or longer.

Opportunities of chance.

However, it was the doors that opened to other things that mattered most to me, and why it was important to keep talking my way into and out of various phases of where I happened to be at the time. Better paying radio jobs for example and ultimately a few that would change me forever. I eventually talked my way out of broadcasting and into an entirely different workplace where I would continue to be paid to talk.

Some of my work as the Public Information Officer for the Franklin County Sheriff's Office is written here, as well as my departure from that and what would eventually move me to the Obetz Police Department where I would retire from working altogether. From working, but not yet from talking my way through what is left.

As others in authority have said to me throughout what has now become a long life, I have some explaining to do. I began doing that a few years ago with a blog I called Life is a Jukebox, and as you read along that will begin to make sense.

Writing became a way of passing time during the early days of my retirement, and as I continued to write about things that seemed worth writing about, I began hearing from the subjects of many of my stories. People I had not thought much about until I started documenting them and their places in my own travels.

A lot of this has to do with my experiences as a paid talker, but much of it is about the city I have lived in all my life, how I used to entertain it, then had to explain it, and later protect it.

I have tried to select a sort of best of essays from not only various blogs, but I have also included pieces from various other journals and diaries I have kept through the years. This publication is not to suggest that I am finished writing about any of this, rather it is more like the beginning and middle of stories still to be shared.

A way of showing the similarities of two very different professions.

So offered in no particular order, here is how I talked my way through it.

Going Home Again

I have written other essays on the topic of trying to go home again. Partly because I have always rejected the idea, that one cannot do it. Moreover, because I have always been a sentimentalist. Sometimes that is a good thing to be, other times it is a very sad thing and I am sure anyone who does not have a sentimental side is probably better off emotionally.

People who either forget, or just do not care about the past have an advantage on those of us who do. If the past is meaningless, than it is smooth sailing into the future. Easier to get where one wants to go.

More money. *More* toys, all adding up to more friends, or a version of what one considers friends.

But then there are people like me. I cannot take one-step forward without remembering where I was. And as I look back, I tend to see only the good stuff. Somehow, I have trained my mind to do this.

What were difficult or horrible events in my life live somewhere in a fog.

Therefore, I guess it was inevitable that I came home to purchase the house I grew up in after my parents passed away. *The House* as it has been frequently referred to is still in the family. The bedroom I used to share with my brother Bob is again the place I sleep, the bathroom door I used to pound on to yell at my sisters Patty and Susie is the same one I pound on now when my wife Mary is in there primping.

And it is here where I will attempt to explain how I did go home again.

Even though everything inside and around the outside of the house is familiar, I find myself thinking about really being home when I go to bed. Maybe because it is at the end of my day and I do not have the distractions that occupy my thoughts most of the other times.

I can walk around the neighborhood that my family has resided in for more than fifty years and still see what used to be here. Cosmetically a lot has changed, homes have been remodeled and some businesses have either left, or have become something else.

American made automobiles that used to dominate the area have all but disappeared and have been replaced by the high price junk made over seas. Most of them ugly, silver cars. The people are not as friendly, and those very few who still live in the area who were here back in the late 1950's and early '60s are either too frail to come out and mingle or are too scared to do so.

The smells that I remember as a kid are also gone, nothing in life ever smelled better to me than the stench of burning leaves in the fall. I even enjoyed the chore of separating trash, putting glass and metal garbage into one can and anything flammable into a fifty gallon drum to burn. Then watching and whiffing little infernos. Early recycling. Do that now and it is a criminal offense.

The neighborhood itself used to smell like produce.

When I was a kid almost everyone had fruit trees in their back yards, or vegetable gardens, or grapes growing on an arbor. Those yards now are dotted with swimming pools, hot tubs and fancy landscaping. And instead of produce, the air often reeks of chlorine.

Columbus history books let us know that 100 years ago this town stunk in another way.

With its factories belching black smoke, (people burning their trash and leaves), the Scioto River with its bouquet' and livestock being delivered to neighborhood slaughter houses. All of that was a part of this area as recently as the early 1960s.

A few people still had chickens in their yards, neighborhood dogs wandered freely, and no one walked them with a retractable leash in one hand and a bag of poop in the other. Dog poop did not seem to be an issue then. Thankfully, some of the yuppies in my neighborhood do carry the bag, while others just leave the poop on my grass and go on. Maybe they are missing the old days too.

Therefore, as progress has changed a lot of that, we became more polite, and the smell of the south end changed. Some of it for the better. However, one thing that has not changed is the sounds of the many trains that crisscross through various neighborhoods, some within a mile of my home.

Back to the bedroom I shared with my brother.

I remember lying in bed as a kid and drifting off to sleep with the sound of train horns off in the distance. I used to wonder where they were going, whether they had passengers, or carried freight. The horns sounded like they were miles away and because my world did not extend much further than a few blocks from the house I guess they were.

And now when I go to bed I hear those familiar sounds, almost on the hour most nights. Distant train horns sounding as they did in 1962. Moreover, when I hear them I really feel that sense of being home.

In no other neighborhood I have lived in did trains sound this familiar.

What is different is they sound closer, and because my world is bigger, I guess they are. Same railroad tracks, closer trains. Therefore, even though many things around me have changed, I know that I did go home again, and the hourly blasts of train horns late at night are a welcome reminder.

Night Moves

In 1974 WNCI Program Director E. Karl told me that a doctor in Westerville was opening a nightclub in Gahanna and had requested me to help establish the clubs entertainment venue. I agreed to meet Doctor Joe Amico at his club on Granville Street and began not only a working relationship, but also a friendship that would last for several years.

Joe had previously operated a movie house on the spot, and had just completed extensive renovations to change it from a *Jerry Lewis Cinema Theatre* to a place where young people could come and dance amid spectacular lighting, ear splitting rock and roll and drink. Cokes mostly, or so we all thought.

What he had envisioned was a nightclub for adults, but because of strong opposition from the Gahanna power structure, he would have to endure months of quibbling for a liquor license. So the *Yellow Lion* opened as a place where high schoolers could congregate until curfew, and get an early jump on the experience of "clubbing."

It was believed, but never proven that some of these kids brought their own liquor to pour into their soft drinks when no one was looking. It was known that many of them found ways to play around in the darkness of the club, and on numerous occasions, I drove someone home who was either too high or too intoxicated to find their own way. Either out of fear of calling their parents to pick them up, or because I had to take their keys. I was the house DJ, and at age 22 only a few years older than these kids.

A lighted marquee in front of the place announced that WNCI was in the house nightly, and it attracted several more clubbers, some in their 20's, sometimes older.

And each time the City of Gahanna tried to block Joes quest for a liquor license I thought, *are these people crazy?* They preferred a nightclub that was open to their teenage sons and daughters, to an adult's only venue.

Good looking out for your kids! It was probably my first experience at watching "Big Brother" go too far.

In their zeal to keep Joe from opening another bar in their community, they were in fact contributing to the delinquency of their own kids. As time went on a liquor license was approved for the Yellow Lion and it became the classiest tavern in Gahanna. That was Joe's ambition.

I stayed with the Amico family for several months dividing my time between the bar and WNCI. And as the place evolved into *Hollywood East*, we started booking nationally known recording artists to replace the records played from the DJ booth.

As I think back to those many months of watching kids grow up too fast, I am reminded that sometimes a community's best intentions to regulate other peoples behavior makes me more determined to keep my own mind clear of wanting to dictate my morals to others. Because, like the leaders of Gahanna back in 1974, I could be wrong.

Midnight Special

By the mid 1970s Bob Smith had become one of the most celebrated stars of radio and television as the legendary Wolfman Jack. His Friday night TV show on NBC, Mid-*Night Special was among the three* hippest programs on the tube sharing the "cool factor" with *Saturday Night Live and Don Kirshner's Rock Concert.*

Wolman's nationally syndicated radio show was on WNCI and it seemed every taxi-cab in Columbus had a neon lighted sign on its roof advertising his program, as well as every COTA bus, and anywhere else the station could advertise.

In 1975 WNCI brought the Wolfman to Columbus for a Valentines Day promotion that was held in the Scotts Inn Motel at Sinclair and Morse Road-also the home of "The Great 98" as it was monikered in the days before digital dial positions. The night that he flew into Port Columbus International Airport I got a call from our Program Director, E. Karl, and he told me to mess up my hair and put on anything with a WNCI logo and get to the airport.

The *Wolf* was due to arrive within the hour.

It was late at night and since I received the call while I was in bed my hair was already a mess, so all I needed to do was to find my cleanest "Go to bed with a friend" t-shirt and make tracks for the terminal. "Go to bed with a friend was the station logo at the time.

When I got the there it was clear that the other 'NCI staffers had gotten the same surprised phone call because we were all wearing different WNCI themed shirts. Some actually had on Wolfman Jack shirts. I felt under-dressed.

When he entered the terminal I remember being in awe of his seemingly bigger than life presence. He was taller than I thought he would be, even a little stockier.

Dressed casually in a blue denim shirt and jeans, wearing turquoise necklaces, bracelets and rings, the man was impressive. Moreover, since it was February it was clear that he came from somewhere sunny, he was tanned, and next to him, we looked pale and sickly. There were not any tanning salons around back then.

I had already met some of our other syndicated superstars, Casey Kasem, Dr. Demento, and Flo and Eddie, who were actually Mark Volman and Howard Kalen of the rock group The Turtles. WNCI carried their syndicated programs as well.

Nevertheless, meeting The Wolfman was special, he was special. I never met anyone as well known around the globe as he was, who anyone who was as down to earth as he appeared to be. The guy was absolutely likeable. But then again so were all of the guys at WNCI, he seemed like one of us.

"Us" included Dave Anthony our mid-day jock who also hosted a Sunday night jazz program, which was another radical idea that Phil Sheridan, our General Manager allowed on his rock station. Our morning guy, Charlie Pickard aka "The Chaz" was considered for years the best production man in the market- Mike Metzger our resident philosopher afternoon drive host, Jay Michaels and "Easy Ed" Hayword and myself rounding out the on-air staff.

Compared to those hippies I was just a kid still honing my craft.

Another member of our radio commune was our Music Director, Damon Sheridan. I was surrounded by the guys who helped WNCI in its early assault to knock off the great and unstoppable WCOL. This by the way was E. Karl's mission in life at that time. He used to say that he would turn 22 South Young Street, the site of the 'COL studios into a parking lot. Today they are sister stations.

The night that Wolfman came to visit us he was taken at his request to

White Castle where he ordered something like thirty burgers. And after ordering, he asked the rest of the guys, "Do you guys want anything?"

Thirty burgers somehow did not seem like enough for a guy like that.

Riders on the Storm

I remember the first time I spent third shift in a Franklin County Sheriff's patrol car getting my first glimpse of people's bad behavior, and how cops deal with it. I was getting ready to jump from the ease of the broadcasting industry where I made my living interviewing newsmakers for four hours each afternoon on WCOL, and into the world some of those newsmakers lived. However, I did not know it yet.

My hair was still long and my attitude toward cops had not yet shifted from suspicious to trust. The idea was to interview a working deputy sheriff, make notes, and craft the experience into a topic for a future radio program.

It seems silly now, but I was truly impressed as I began to observe police work up close and personal for the first time.

Impressed at the job cops are faced with, on what I was learning was a routine workday for them. What seemed to be a big deal for me was just another day at the office for Deputy Claire Betzko, the patrol officer I rode with that night.

When I showed up as scheduled at the Sheriff's patrol bureau on Mound Street next to Cooper Stadium, I met the "C" Company Lieutenant, Tom Haines.

Lt. Haines was not too thrilled to see me, and seemed reluctant to allow me to even do the *ride along*, but he was gracious and placed me with Deputy Betzko.

Claire also had reservations about having someone from the media riding as a passenger all-night, watching him and asking questions, but he went along with it and within minutes of pulling out of the sub station I had convinced him that I was only there to observe, that I would not interfere with his work and that I would make him a radio star.

Before the first hour went by, I felt like I knew the guy.

Claire, or "Butch" as he was known by other Deputies was a great subject to observe. He was tough, smart and was nothing like any television cop I had ever watched on the tube; as a matter of fact, he made fun of them most of the night.

He was a career Army Ranger who was probably trained in every way a man can be to settle bad situations. He was a quiet guy who took his work seriously, and riding along and seeing his routine, I thought it was similar to the first time I sat in a radio station watching Beemon J. Black at WCOL work his on-air magic. Similar in that I began thinking, this looks like fun!

*Beemon was the DJ who jump-started my radio career; I will discuss him often as we go along.

I knew the night I met Claire that I was going to accept Sheriff Earl O. Smith's offer to become his Public Information Officer, even if it meant shaving, cutting my hair and spending the next several months attending the Sheriff's Training Academy.

Following that first night experience Claire and I became very good friends, we remained friends throughout my law enforcement career. He was someone I could always count on. His family and mine did some things together, his wife and mine became friends, and even after I left the Sheriff's Office for a job with the Obetz Police Department he would find himself in my jurisdiction offering any assistance he could provide.

The last time I spoke to him was shortly before I retired. Someone once said to me, "Life can turn on a dime." Mine did a few times. One turn into the WCOL studios on South Young Street, another into the sheriff's sub station on Mound Street.

Hello it's me

Every disc jockey has had to perform at one time or another at a school dance, a class reunion or a wedding. I did this more times than I want to remember. At first, I would spin records at these events because I needed the extra money that could be earned doing it. Later in life I did it because friends expected it. Either for their own shindigs or for someone close to them.

But I can honestly say that I hated every minute of doing those things. Spinning tunes in a studio was a blast, regardless of the format I was involved with, but when doing it for groups of people in a VFW hall or a gymnasium, it sucked. As an emcee, you try to make people believe you are enjoying their shenanigans, but I never did.

Weddings were the worst.

At wedding receptions you have to please all demographics, forget the bride and groom, you have to also please all of the little kids who pester you to play whatever the top two teeny-bop songs are on the charts, and they will want them played over and over. And the young adults whose tastes might run anywhere between head-banging rock, country& western, hip-hop and Bohemian Waltzes, and then their are the grand parents and their friends, who would prefer that you stick with a play list of 1930s and 1940s music.

I could always expect someone asking me to play the occasional

Black Sabbath or Jimi Hendrix tunes, and when I did the elderly people would shoot dirty looks and give hand signals to turn it down.   As the person charged with providing the sound track for the event you are almost always screwed.

The worst part of the night comes when you have to play the special song for the father-daughter dance, usually something saccharine like "Daddy's Little Girl."

Then another one for the brides mother to dance with the groom, something for the bride and her new father-in-law, something for the best man and the bridesmaid, it all gets pretty sickening.

And finally, there is that needle in the ear for the happy couple.

"We've Only Just Begun" comes to mind. Torture. And before the end of the day everyone wants to dance to those cool novelty things like "The Chicken Dance" "The Macarena" "Strokin'" and every other obnoxious melody that gets requested at *ALL weddings.*

It is enough to make a DJ want to puke, or at least beg his away out of any such obligation. I finally learned to say no. The last wedding I hosted was for a friend, and like every other one I ever did, it was more miserable than the one before it.

However, my worst memory of emceeing a social event was one that nearly got me killed.

It was 1974 and I was sent by the WNCI Program Director, E. Karl to host a school dance for Marion River Valley High School. It was a winter dance party on a Saturday night. At the time, I was the stations all-night DJ so anything I did before my midnight shift would be something I would do with very little sleep. I was to be paid $200.00 so in a way it was okay.

The day of the dance, I loaded up the WNCI van with sound equipment, in those days it was turntables for the records, an amplifier the size of a small refrigerator, speakers taller than me, a few party lights, a microphone and miles of chords.

The dance was scheduled to start at 7:00 PM so I scooted up the freeway around 5:30. About half way to Marion the snow became almost blinding, it was getting nearly impossible to see the road, let alone stay on it.

As I got closer to my destination, I could see a railroad crossing ahead with a fast moving train crossing the road. I panicked and hit the brakes, and because I was on ice, the van went where it wanted to go. Off the road and into a ditch.

This caused everything in the truck to slide forward, crashing into the back of the seat, the dashboard and into me. It took awhile but I was able to get back on the road and I did make it to the dance, about 8:00. When I got there, I was met by the nastiest female I had ever been verbally attacked by. She was more than a little pissed because I was late.

I don't know if she was a parent, a teacher or the school mascot, but she was not pleased that my arrival was the opposite of prompt. She clearly wanted to smack me. Regardless, with the help of a few students I unpacked my gear anyway and set it up in the gym.

When I plugged it all in, nothing worked.

Apparently, my ditch mishap had broken some things. So we improvised. The students raided the schools audio-visual aids closet, brought out two very old record players, and plugged me into the schools public address system, and by 9:00, the kids were dancing. And they danced until 9:30, the scheduled time for the events conclusion.

When it was over the woman who had chastised me earlier for being late, told me to pack up my junk and get out. So I packed it, loaded it all back into the truck and went back inside to ask for my money. Thinking I had just earned two hundred bucks for a half hour performance I was thinking the night went well.

Instead, after being dressed down verbally for not providing what was promised I left without being paid anything.

Funds I had counted on, especially since the needle on the vans gas gauge was in the danger zone, and I had not thought to take any money with me. Not my brightest plan. Nevertheless, I did make it back to I-71 and Morse Road by 11:30, which under other circumstances would have been enough time to be there for the start of my show at twelve.

The problem was the van ran out of gas on the exit ramp from the freeway to Morse Road.

The WNCI studios were on Sinclair Road about two blocks from Morse, so I left the vehicle on the side of the road and walked to work, arriving only about twenty minutes late. Because I did have a few friends in Columbus I made arrangements for someone to get the van back to the 'NCI parking lot.

Oddly as it seemed in the years that passed, Marion River Valley High School never again invited me back.

I would like to forget it as much as they would, and I suspect there are some who came to dance that night who still harbor less than fond memories of my visit when they think back. Especially when the class of '74 goes hunting for a DJ to host their reunions.

Watching Scottie Grow

After being hired away from WCOL by Sheriff Earl O. Smith I returned to my old broadcasting stomping grounds as a weekend DJ and morning traffic reporter.

In the late 1980's, the 92X morning show consisted of an eclectic group of personalities including Tom Kelly, who was often off the wall, sports nut Mark "The Shark" Howell, prissy and innocent little Kelly Quinn and one of the zaniest personalities in Columbus at that time, Scott McKenzie.

Scott brought to 92X that big radio market style of wit and wisdom, and was the perfect fit for that show. I was their traffic reporter. Or, the guy who struggled to report something serious among jesters.

My own reports were a joke, they had less to do with reasons traffic moved slowly through the capital city than they were an opportunity to make fun of something I could never stand to hear on a radio show.

I still hate hearing traffic reports.

My own history as a radio announcer was in trying to make people smile and hopefully be entertained, and here I was, expected to play radio cop, and help motorists navigate traffic jams. It was hard to take this role seriously. So I did what I had to do, I made up the reports and with the help of the 92x morning guys they were often more humorous than informative.

They were somewhat accurate, and had we taped them back then they could be replayed today, and still be somewhat accurate. Anyone listening did not need Dick Geary or me, or Bill Taylor at Sunny 95 to tell them where the slowdowns were. It is always slow going around the hospital curve on Rt. 315 near Riverside Hospital, slow coming up from the South on I-71, and slower as you approach the 70-71-315 split.

Don't believe it? Listen to traffic reports any morning, on any station in Columbus now. I told you about the same slowdowns in the '80's that you will hear about tomorrow.

The traffic has not sped up since then on I-70 coming in from the eastside, especially as you got near the Livingston Avenue curve. Still a bottleneck every morning during rush hour. That part of the reporting was easy.

It would be easy today.

As for knowing where the accidents that caused slow downs were, I monitored Dick over at WMNI and plagiarized his information. The challenge was to make it interesting.

I had a lot of help from my *supporting staff* on the 92X morning show.

That's right, I thought of it as "Morning Traffic with Deputy Rick" starring Tom Kelly, Kelly Quinn, Mark Howell and Scott McKenzie, with a little rock & roll music in the background. These people would *not* let me do a serious traffic report even if I wanted to.

They played the Batman theme under my reports, sound effects of screeching tires and cars crashing, and then lead into the segments with back and forth banter that made it nearly impossible for me to say anything with a straight face or with any sense of seriousness.

On the first warm morning of a spring day following a bitterly cold winter, I had to do a traffic report on the back up on Broad Street in front of the station caused by two of my team mates, who decided to celebrate the thaw by standing on the corner of Broad and Fourth Street stripped to their underwear.

They had taken some remote equipment outside where they could broadcast from out there, and as they waved and shouted at passing traffic, cars were stopping and blowing their horns, all the while the guys were asking me on the air, "How's the traffic on Broad Street?"

When I finished my morning duties at the station I went to my own office at the sheriff's department where by then, there was a rumor circulating that the entire morning crew at 92X had been on Broad Street in their underwear.

Before the end of the day, the sheriff had heard it, and asked me if I had participated in that stunt. I had to explain that my only participation was remaining behind in the studios as the voice of reason, and reporting on the chaos it caused.

A female deputy who was a regular listener of ours, having driven through the area and seeing them in their underwear that morning commented - "They sound bigger on the radio."

Sideshow

Hosting a talk show was probably the most worthwhile thing I did as a broadcaster. Playing music was fun, but nothing really meaningful came from many years as a disc jockey other than having a lot of fun, and maybe establishing myself as an announcer. It was in talk radio where I think I finally caught up to what broadcasters should be doing.

As it turned out, it changed not only my outlook on the business, but the business I went into as a result; law enforcement. Had I not met Sheriff Earl O. Smith when I did, I might have spent the next twenty years chasing radio signals.

I doubt if I would have enjoyed the tenure that guys like Bob Conners of WTVN and Mark Wagner of WLVQ have had, by remaining gainfully employed by the same employer for as many years as they have.

I have written about some of the more memorable experiences I had in radio, and some of the more interesting interviews I did. Earl Smith topping the list as the best, certainly the most important.

However, three stand out as miserable attempts to bond with a guest.

I thought Vincent Bugliosi who prosecuted Charles Manson for the famous Tate/Labianca murders in 1969 was a bit of an ass. I could not get much past the introduction with him. It was my hope to discuss the Manson Family and somehow our signals got crossed.

He did not want to talk about it, and within five minutes of the conversation, he was suggesting that I was incompetent, which was the least of his insults before he hung up on me.

Next on the forgettable list was Mike Ferrell, aka B.J. Hunnicutt from the TV show-M*A*S*H. I was under the impression that we would talk a little about that show and some of the characters that were on it.

He wanted to discuss something else, and was clearly annoyed when I kept trying to steer him into that conversation. He too ended the discussion rather abruptly when it became clear that he was not going to control it. Another dial tone in my ear.

And then there was Goober, known in the real world as George Lindsey. The only thing I found interesting about him was his years on "The Andy Griffith Show" and his time spent as a cast member on the country and western variety show, "Hee Haw."

And that was what I wanted to chat about, I wanted to hear about Barney and Andy, but I also wanted to talk about Buck Owens and Roy Clark and what it was like to work with that corny cast.

But Goober wanted to spend the hour talking about "The Andy Griffith Reunion Show," a program that was scheduled to be on television that night. He thought we had booked him to do an hour-long promo for the show.

Each time I tried to steer him back to the "Hee Haw" he became more and more irritated. Finally, *I* ended the conversation.

Doing talk radio changed how I looked at celebrities. I used to get excited about opportunities to meet them, but that slowly changed. I became someone who would rather not meet them. I found that it was better to admire them from afar, by watching them on television, or hearing them on the radio or by reading things they published.

If you never meet someone you have high opinions of, you probably won't ever be disappointed by them.

After meeting Goober, I really missed Gomer, the character he replaced, and after my chat with Mike Ferrell, I remembered how much funnier Trapper John was when he was Hawkeye's bunkmate. Moreover, Vincent Bugliosi had me, at least for a moment, rooting for Manson's acquittal the next time I watched Helter Skelter.

But only for a moment.

Life Is a Rock but the Radio Rolled Me

When sharing old radio stories it is not easy for me to leave out some of the best chapters. However, I have not found a polite way to craft the words to write the "Best Of" series yet. Partly because some of the best stuff involves many peoples three favorite sins, but I will take a shot.

Some of the more graphic stories that can be written involve DJ's having sex while on the air, without screwing up their show, and some who could not pull it off, but tried anyway.

In one scenario, a program director who was hoping for affection from an overnight female DJ for a while walked into her studio one night, stripped off all of his clothing, and stood naked and attempted to make a deal with her. It did not work out as he had hoped it would.

Probably hoping he was arousing her he instead repulsed her.

He should have gone to jail for the stunt, but not only did he not get arrested; he somehow managed to turn the tables and make himself look like the victim. He was never held accountable, and the station management allowed the incident to just sort of pass.

The DJ victim left not only the company, but the state of Ohio as well. Had she chosen to do so she could have brought about serious legal challenges to both the PD and the owners of the station.

Another incident involves my friend Jim Davis while we were working at WMNI.

Jim was our resident superstar at the time.

One afternoon a stripper from the nightclub *40 Carats,* which was located across the street from our Southern Hotel studios, came to the station pretending to want to meet Jim.

Our Program Director, Steve Cantrell and our Sales Manager, Jim Rapp told her that Jim was on the air and could not be bothered.

As it turned out, they were right.

She told them she was sure *she could* bother him if she were permitted to strip naked and walk in on him. They agreed to let her, but gave specific instructions that she would have to go in while the "on-air" light was on, and while Jim was busy reading sports.

So as Jim went on the air for a three-minute sports report she entered the studio, naked, and sat on his lap.

Without breaking his flow, he delivered his report flawlessly.

When he finished, she asked him (on the air) if there was anything on his mind.

Jim replied "Yes, now that you've brought it up, I just remembered, my wife asked me to bring home a quart of milk." Everyone in the building busted out laughing.

Another Davis story;

There was a pain in the ass that used to call Jim every night and ask for a certain record she wanted played. She also wanted to come to the station to meet him, but he was leery and always made excuses to avoid any such encounters.

One day she showed up anyway and she was a mess.

She looked like she had slept under a bridge. She was dirty; she filled the room with stench, and was one of the homeliest women I had ever seen. When she told me who she was, I told her that Jim was dying to meet her. So I waited for the on-air light to come on and told her to just go into the studio and meet him.

Jim was talking on the air and you could hear her making background noises and talking loudly, shouting actually, "Hi Jim!" "Whatcha doin?"

Jim was hearing the chaos behind him as he tried to maintain his composure, and when he finished his bit, he turned around, took one look and ran out of the studio where I was and asked, "What the Hell is that?"

I told him who she was and he walked toward the restroom and said, "Get her the Hell out of here!" He was laughing so hard I could tell he enjoyed it as much as I did. When he did return to the studio, he was still laughing, and he was carrying a can of air freshener, after emptying it he looked at me and said, "You son of a bitch, I thought someone had brought me a fish sandwich!"

That night he must have called me a son of a bitch a dozen more times, and each time he said it, it sounded funnier than the last time. Jim could cuss and laugh aloud at the same time.

Moving across town to WTVN several years earlier.

There was a particular DJ there that a few of us did not care for. We thought he was pompous and full of himself, and he was one of those guys who would not think twice about screwing one of us any chance he had.

The custom for a DJ who was going off the air was to make the studio ready for the jock coming on. One of the courtesies we did for the replacement was to stack up his first hour of commercial cartridges in the order they were to be played.

This one particular DJ who was leaving WTVN for a radio station across town decided to take one last parting shot, by switching the labels of some of this guys commercials. That is, if the log called for a Lazarus commercial he might play a Dodge commercial. On the other hand, there might not be a commercial on that tape, it might be a long obnoxious fart sound, or disgusting belch sound effect, anything but what the label said it was.

Sun TV? Rite Rug?

No. After his opening remarks welcoming listeners to his show, the announcer said, "I'll be back after this." Then all Hell broke loose. When he hit the button hoping to play a commercial, he farted. Or was it the tape?

He hit the next button and his listeners heard the longest belch ever recorded.

Trying to maintain his composure he came back on the air and said, "Okay, someone's playing games" and when he started the next series of "spots" he aired a compilation of spliced commercials for other products.

One was asking, "Do you have jock itch?" Then by the magic of over-dubbing a baby could be heard crying then quickly interrupted by "My hemorrhoids are killing me" then a few more fart sounds followed by an announcer saying "Use only as directed" ending with a jingle that sang the station call-letters and the jocks name, followed by another fart and another long belch.

After what sounded less than a heartfelt apology, he began to ramble something about "children should not be allowed in radio studios without strict parental supervision." That was followed by nearly a half minute of dead air as he scrambled to get a record on the turntable.

Between practical jokes, slips of the tongue and just plain bad behavior, a lot of us paid some hefty dues along the way.

Including myself.

While working at WMNI one night I received a call from a guy who identified himself as Merle Haggard's manager.

He gave the right name, and the right hotel where Merle was staying while in town for a concert, so I was eager to do it when he asked if I would like to promote the show by interviewing Haggard on the air.

I called my program director to get permission and he told me to go for it.

So the manager arranged for me to call his room, which I did, and for the next hour, I conducted my interview. During commercial breaks, he and I would talk off the air, and he kept asking if I could fix him up with a girl, two or more if I could get them, someone who would spend time with him in his hotel room.

That was no problem because my phones were ringing off the hook from listeners wanting to talk to him, and it was not uncommon in those days for frisky women to call radio stations late at night.

As this went on my friend, Tiny Wellman, a well-known country singer in the area called me and said he was suspicious. Tiny said, "It does sound like him, but I can't be sure." Wellman suspected the guy was an imposter.

He suggested that I ask him about his role in a TV show that was airing that week, a made for TV mini series called "The Sentenial" which Haggard was starring in.

So when I came back from a break I asked my guest if he wanted to talk about his television role, he replied, "What television role?"

Oops.

When I told him the name of the show, he told me he had not seen that one.

I quickly thanked him for his time and ended the interview. I put on a real Merle Haggard record and got back on the phone to threaten his life. He was laughing and he confided that he was really another jock from across town. It turned out that he was calling from a hotel, and I had given his room number to at least two girls.

Later in the show, one of them called me back screaming all sorts of expletives accusing me of setting her up. She had gone to the hotel looking to hook up with a country music superstar but only found a horny local DJ.

The other girl never called back, and the DJ who set me up never called to thank me for making his night. I did get a call from the Program Director. He told me it was a great interview. I wanted to tell him the truth. However, some things are left better unsaid. That was one of those things.

Heartbreak Hotel

When I first went to work at WMNI, the station was not yet 20 years old. To put that in perspective, I have been around 5 years longer than those blinking towers in Grove City along Marlane Drive just off I-71.

In retrospect, I guess I did not think about such things when I was in my mid twenties. The studios we worked out of at The Great Southern Hotel and the equipment we used had to be older than the towers and me.

Our control console, turntables and tape recorders were like dinosaurs when compared to the equipment I had used earlier in stints at WTVN and WNCI.

Listeners of WMNI could not have known that because our station sounded great.

Old tape recordings of my own show sound better than I ever did. Station President and General Manager, Bill Mnich even came into the studio once and offered advice on how to work on my voice, to bring it down from sounding like a tenor to something more manly.

I never thought of myself as a tenor. Mnich himself had that "mans" voice. One of the deepest I ever heard. One that could shake a room. The voice exercises he suggested actually worked and before my second, of about six years there I noticed a difference. On the other hand, maybe I just thought I did.

Throughout this book I have written about my own life and times with WMNI and I have often said those were probably my best years in radio.

Decades have passed since I left the station and since WMNI moved out of the hotel to their studios on Dublin Road, but I cannot go through the intersection of South High Street and East Main Street without looking up at that building, and have the memories flooding back as if they were mere weeks ago.

Today the station couldn't sound more different with his adult standards format than it did when Loretta Lynn and Conway Twitty helped me make friends, get laid and take my mind off of the personal struggles of being broke, in debt, getting married, divorced and remarried.

Friends I met then are some of the best I have still today. Moreover, Bill's surviving family members still treat me like one of their own anytime our paths cross. I will forever miss Mr. Mnich and the opportunities he gave me when he took a chance by hiring me, at first for three dollars an hour because as he said, I was coming in with experience.

Forty Miles of Bad Road

When I was just a few years younger than I am now I used to go with my dad to Chillicothe, Ohio on weekend fishing trips and for visits with his family. We only made that trip in three different cars. First, a 1956 Ford Customline that my dad bought new, later a 1964 Ford Fairlaine and later in his new 1973 Ford Torino, listening to the AM car radio there and back.

I can remember on those trips down Route 23 from Columbus being told by my dad that after we got out of the city limits we would be traveling 40 miles of bad road to be with genuine people. My Dad was a country boy from down there and thought people in Columbus were extravagant, probably a little weird.

He made it sound like we were embarking on a road trip. Trips that far South for me still are road trips. I do not travel well. Being the radio buff I've been most of my life I remember on the way down passing a little station in Circleville, that back then would have been a perfect subject for a Norman Rockwell painting. It was WNRE.

It sat alongside Rt. 23 by itself with its broadcasting tower just steps from its tiny building. It reminded me of WBEX in Chillicothe; I used to imagine working there one day. I never gave it any thought that I would be working for, and with people who started their radio careers in that region .

Bill Mnich worked in Chillicothe when he was young and he brought Carl Wendelken to Columbus from there. Others would eventually follow. Carl was a fixture at WMNI for about three decades.

Another announcer from there was a girl named Tonda Vanover. The first female DJ on the WMNI block. Tight jeans, a cowboy hat and boots, she showed up in a black, Smokey and the Bandit Trans AM and with an attitude that matched her car. She called herself Cherokee.

A gifted announcer and a good fit for our format. As she would say, a little bit country and a little bit watch yourself.

I have lost touch with nearly everyone from that era except business guru Eddie Powell who has remained closely tied with local broadcasting. Eddie was a kid who began showing up at the station as a friend of a friend of mine. He became our nighttime announcer and a life-long comrade. Immersing himself in everything from square dance calling, hosting television shows, live concerts, motivational speaking, teaching and a host of other adventures.

His book, "How to Get the Job You Have Always Dreamed Of" accents a career of helping others find work and fine-tune business adventures. Then there was Joe Higman a guy with a big heart to match his physical frame.

A gentle giant. One of the nicest people in radio, and the guy who grabbed the console for me when I had to abandon my radio show one night to rush to Mt. Carmel Hospital for the birth of my son Kevin.

After I got the new arrival to sleep, and the nurses and the baby's mother settled down, I returned to the station to relieve him but I nearly had to wrestle the microphone away from him. He insisted I go home and get rested. He genuinely cared.

Just a few from a good group of announcers from the 1970's through the mid '80's who were like a family. Albeit dysfunctional at times, we all left lasting impression not only on our listeners, but also with each other. Good, bad or indifferent, impressions.

The Name Game

Ex WBEX radio man Larry Roberts was Chillicothe's version of our Doctor Bop, the famous DJ who launched a radio revolution in Columbus back in the 1950's. Like Doc, Larry was introducing Chillicothe, Ohio to rock & roll back then.

He played the first rock & roll record on the radio down there about the same time it was being introduced in Columbus.

Had I known about his past when I used to watch him anchor the news here on channel 4 I would have paid closer attention to his newscasts. This guy's resume makes my own look empty.

Reading his abbreviated bio I've learned that he hung out with some of the people I met along my own journey, like Roy Orbison, Gary Lewis and the Playboy's, the Turtles and Rick Derringer, but he met these guy's when they were in their prime.

I caught up with a few of them during their nostalgic tours.

Then of course, there was The Beatles. Larry interviewed them three times, and was in on the Toronto interview with Lennon over the Jesus controversy.

I was only seven years old in the late 1950's when Larry was doing his thing but I am hoping some of his radio past is locked somewhere in my sub-conscience. I hope to someday unlock that thing and review what might be stored in it. That is, I may have heard him on the radio when I was a kid going back and forth to Chillicothe on those trips I mentioned.

When I talk to Larry now he mentions people like Maurice Jackson, the long-ago morning voice at WTVN. Johnny Dollar who I knew as Jim Pidcock the sales manager when I worked there in the early and mid 1970's. Roberts knew them all, including my old friend Dave Logan another WBEX alumnus.

It is strange to think of the many connections I have to former WBEX personalities that have made their way up North. Strange for example to think of the smooth talking, laid back Dave Logan from WTVN playing rock music years before I met him.

Other people Larry knew include the late Jim Runyon from WTVN, Rod Serling (The Twilight Zone) and Jonathan Winters who both worked at WBNS and Nick Clooney from WLWC who brought his young son George to work with him when he was just a toddler.

I have all the respect in the world for Spook Beckman, one of the most remembered personalities in Columbus broadcast history, another of Larry's friends, and if Spook were alive I would love to be in the same room with the two of them and listen to them exchange stories.

The Night They Drove
Old Dixie Down

This is a tribute to my good friends at the Columbus Police Department who worked "C' Company, (third shift) several years ago when I was an Obetz Police patrolman assigned to the 10:00 PM to 6:00 AM shift.

Law enforcement officers, regardless of the color of their uniform or the badge on their breast are a close fraternity of people. Something called "Mutual Aid" kept a lot of us working for various departments very close. Under the Mutual Aid Pact it was not uncommon for Franklin County Sheriff's Deputies, State Troopers, Groveport Police, Madison Township officer's and occasionally even a cop from the Brice PD or Lithopolis to back each other up in what we called "Zone Four." And of course, our friends from the Columbus Division of Police.

While patrolling the streets of Obetz I knew more deputies than I did from the other departments primarily because I worked with a number of them for about ten years before trading the black shirt for a blue one.

Nevertheless, there were some good guys from CPD who often "hid" from their supervisors down in our little bailey wick. I won't name them because there is a chance they are still sipping caffeine at the Sunoco on

Alum Creek Drive. A call most cops would rather not get is to check out a suspicious person, probably drunk and grossing people out in an all-night convenience store.

I used to get those occasionally and it usually meant putting some stinky character with a belligerent attitude in the back seat of my cruiser and taking him either to jail, to a psychiatric unit or home, if he had one. Then I would spend a good part of my shift cleaning up crap and fumigating the inside of my patrol car.

Just a few of the reasons most cops do not like those dispatches.

On one such occasion, I was dispatched to a "Duke" gas station to deal with a guy who was hassling customers and causing a disturbance. When I got there, he was drunk, his shirt was covered with vomit and his pants were soaked with his own urine. At least I believed it was his. When I asked him for his identification he had none, but he said his friends just called him "Dixie." He also said I could call him that if I was nice to him.

After an interview that should have taken only two minutes, I learned over the next half hour that he had been walking along Parsons Avenue when he was stopped and questioned by two Columbus Police officer's in a Paddy Wagon.

He told me they asked him if he wanted to go to jail or if he would rather be taken to Obetz. He said he tried to tell them that he would rather be taken home because he was only about two blocks from his house when they picked him up. So home not being on the table he chose the second option. They drove him to my jurisdiction and dropped him off for me to get to know. I knew who these officers were so I gave him a similar option. I asked if he would rather be taken to jail or to his home. He chose the latter.

As I headed north, he became confrontational. Calling me and all cops a bunch of pigs and other unpleasant names. When he started spitting on the glass screen separating me from him I decided I had had enough and that it would be jail instead of his home.

I pulled my cruiser over next door to his house and notified our radio room that I needed a city car to respond to a drunk causing a disturbance. I ordered this clown out of my cruiser and stood with him until CPD arrived. It was not the two who had brought me this problem but they had white shirts and that is all that mattered.

After a few exchanges between myself and them about whose problem he was, I reminded them that I did not have any charges on him and as far as I was concerned he was now in their jurisdiction, therefore he was their problem. I got back into my cruiser and returned to Obetz never knowing whether the guy went into his house or if my buddies from CPD made other arrangements.

Thinking that was the end of that it was only a matter of a few days when I got the same call, but to a different location and for a different drunk with the same story. One would have to work in that environment to see the humanity involved in this sort of thing. At least someone cared enough to bring these problems to someone with the ability to get them to a safe place, and someone with a sense of humor.

Everybody Loves a Clown

Ever wonder what made Flippo one of the most remembered personalities of our generation? Growing up in this area through the 1960's and '70's everyone knew who he was.

From early on when every thing on television was black and white until we could see that the clown suit was blue. That suit by the way is now on display where it should be in a glass case at the Ohio Historical Center. Flippo himself was historical.

"The Clown" as everyone called him, was one of the funniest people around, on or off camera.

Back in the early 1990's while I was still with WCOL-FM the station hired Flippo to be a part of the morning show on Thursdays with Michael Cruise and Kelly Quinn. He literally took over that program. Had he wanted to, he probably could have taken over any morning show in Columbus.

Unlike a lot of morning radio personalities, Flippo's brand of humor was natural. He did not need writers or planners; he just had that gift to crack people up every time he answered a question or posed his own. I don't know if WCOL could have afforded to have him host that show on a daily basis, or if he'd have done it if he were asked. However, it would have been great to keep him around for a few more years.

My own personal favorite recollection of him came back in the late

1980's. I was having lunch at Phillips Coney Island on West Broad Street with a guy who was a "snitch" and had offered information to be delivered to Sheriff Earl Smith. The sheriff did not like the guy so when I told him he had requested a meeting Earl told me to meet him. He said the guy was a habitual liar and he was not going to waste his time. Therefore, I wasted mine, though it was amusing.

As it turned out he did not have anything that the Sheriff wanted to hear, but what he did have that day turned out to be something very big a few years later. This guy was connected to some heavy hitters involved in organized crime. Earl called him the "Tax Man for the Porn Dealers."

As he and I were having lunch, a very good-looking girl came into the diner and took a seat at the counter. She wore a short skirt, had long blonde hair and looked to be in her early twenties. My lunch mate nearly dropped his wiener when he saw her.

He said "I know her, she works for so-and-so." He said she was, in his words, "A West Side Dirty Butt." Meaning she was a hooker. He walked over to speak to her and she blew him off saying that she was waiting for someone. Another guy in the diner tried and he too was ignored. Then Flippo came in and sat down beside her.

We watched as they ate lunch and seemed to carry on a normal conversation between two people who knew each other, and my "new friend" became more and more irritated. He said something like "I can't believe I'm being cock-blocked by Flippo." I am not sure what he meant by that but it sounded funny.

After enjoying his lunch, Flippo left without her. He got into a little red car and drove away. (It was not his familiar one-door Isetta that we grew up watching him climb out of on The Early Show). It was a small Chevy.

Shortly before he died, I attended a tribute to him celebrating his birthday and his long, amazing career. Moreover, I think everyone knew that his name was Bob Marvin, but I never heard anyone call him Bob.

That day when hundreds of people showed up to honor him I heard some of the best "Flippo" stories ever, and even those who enjoyed long careers working with him showed him the respect of addressing him as Flippo. Calling him Bob would have seemed like an insult.

Different Drum

Whenever someone would say something to me like "I would not have your job for all of the money in the world" (speaking of my job as a police officer) I would look at them and think," If you only knew."

For me, hard work and being a police officer had little in common. I spent equal time in both of my careers, law enforcement and broadcasting, and I can tell you that playing records and talking on the radio was a lot harder than the daily routine of filling out paper-work, blowing a whistle while waving at traffic or simply driving a police car for eight hours a day.

Not to diminish the importance of the job, but every cop knows their work is not hard, it can be difficult, but anyone with good common sense, the ability to read, write and understand both, has good community relations skills as well as being able to learn new skills quickly, can make split second decisions and be willing to take chances-some of them that might maim or kill them, can do this job. Sounds like a lot doesn't it?

The bottom line is most cops are born with those qualities. Not all of them, I have known some pretty stupid people who found their way into this profession.

Nevertheless, for most of them, police officers are generally bright people doing a job for the right reasons. They like it.

All young recruits say they want to be a police officer because they want to help people. That is the right thing to say of course, but in all my years as a cop, I knew very few who got into the business for that reason. I have heard most of them say it and I expect e-mails on this topic. But all of the cops I knew chose the work because of the adventure. If wanting to help people was the underlying reason they could have joined the Peace Corp or the Red Cross.

Aside from willing to risk their personal safety for others, and seeing the worst side of those in your community or sharing the grief of crime and accident victims, the work itself is easy. It is the training that is difficult. Whereas in broadcasting it is the opposite.

Both jobs are constantly under public scrutiny and have deep political complications. A broadcaster survives on his ratings, talent and his popularity with management, while police officers survive on their training, fate and their popularity with management. Be it higher-ups in the chain of command, or the politicians who control their purse strings.

Both are constantly criticized. A broadcaster, if he says something others disagree with or plays the wrong music, cops if they issue someone a citation, lock someone up or are spotted taking a break. I know not all cops share my sentiments. For some their job may be the hardest work they have ever done.

For those people I feel sorry for them and would suggest the Peace Corp or the Red Cross as an alternative to help people.

But for me it was the easiest. After I figured out how to make sense of the Ohio Revised Code, got used to taking *shit* from the public and from my bosses, and honed the skills I was taught in the training academy, the job was a breeze.

It was like that for me in broadcasting. I was very lucky to work in two worlds where I enjoyed my work. In nearly 40 years in the combined fields I worked most holidays, most weekends and nearly every birthday and special occasions of all of my family members. I would not have done that if I didn't enjoy my work.

Doctor My Eyes

Everyone knows where they were when they heard that JFK had been murdered. Same when they heard about the Space Shuttle Challenger when it blew up and on September 11, 2001 when the towers fell, the Pentagon was attacked and a United Airliner went down in Pennsylvania.

I also remember where I was and what I was doing when I first realized I needed glasses. No big deal if not for the circumstances. I was in my cruiser one night and I had pulled over a traffic violator.

Whatever I stopped him for was a serious enough offense that I could not let him go with a warning; I had to write him a citation. Prior to this one instance, I had written two or three just a few hours earlier. I had also written a few reports and had kept pace with filling out my nightly activity log.

However, when I looked at this guys Ohio Drivers License, I could not make any of it out. It looked like it had been soaked in water, covered with ink smears. But so did my log sheet and every other piece of printed paper. I got on the radio and called for " back-up." When another officer arrived I handed him the license and asked if he could read it to me, line by line, slowly so I could write the ticket.

I explained that something had happened and although I could see everything else all right, I could not read anything. After issuing the guy the citation I went to a Duke gas station and purchased a small magnifying glass so I would be able to complete any other paper work that I might have the rest of the night.

This was all very strange because up to that moment normal sized printing, including everything on a driver's license was never a challenge. Later that day I bought a pair of reading glasses and within days I had an appointment with an optometrist. I have been lost without prescription glasses since.

A sign then that my working days were coming to a closer ending.

Running On Empty

In 1989 I had one of those schedules I would probably need if I were still working in today's economy. In a sense I was working three jobs, all connected to the Franklin County Sheriff's Office. Some days it became four jobs. And I kept this pace for about a year.

My full time job was as Public Information Officer for the Franklin County S.O., but I had returned to WCOL AM and WXGT-FM (92X) as the morning traffic reporter which meant my week days began at 5:30 AM. "Deputy Rick" as they called me, or as 92X's Tom Kelly would occasionally introduce me, "Deputy Dick."

Following the morning radio show at 22 South Young Street, I hustled over to my office at the Sheriff's department at 370 South Front Street at 9:00 for my 9 to five daily mayhem. Then, about three days a week, I would suit up for special duty at the old Greenbrier apartment complex at James Road and Allegheny Avenue. That assignment was generally from 6:00 PM until midnight, and sometimes later.

In addition to all of this, I was on-call 24 hours each day, all seven of them to handle media relations for high profile events, such as homicides, rapes, serious vehicle crashes or any other gathering place for news reporters. And finally, I hosted a weekend "oldies" program on Saturday's and Sunday's.

I literally did not sleep in 1989. I probably smoked three packs of cigarette's each day and consumed more than a dozen cups of coffee daily, as well as pop breaks, and fast foods with candy sugar rushes between meals. But I never got sick that year, or if I did, I was too tired to care.

By the end of 1989, I had earned a perfect attendance award. I got that six times, but that one was the most special of them all. I could not even take a day off for a vasectomy. I got that during my lunch hour one afternoon and returned to the office immediately following the surgery.

Okay, it was an in-and-out minor surgical procedure. But that day when I got back to my office, Sheriff Earl Smith was in one of his "Where is my PIO moods."

When I told him how I spent my lunch hour, he told me to go home. I could not do that because we had a serious incident while I was away and reporters were lining up across the hall where our detective bureau was. Plus I wanted that perfect attendance award.

Looking back, I made a lot of money that year. By the end of it, I was still deep in debt. I was married to a shopper. I was living proof that the more you make the more you spend. Make that, the more *someone* spends.

These days are not so hectic. And even though writing this book is a lot easier than living what is in it, I still miss cruising in the passing lane sometimes; I did a lot of driving back then. And someday I will get a tune-up and get back out there. For now, I will just keep both hands on the keyboard.

Young Hearts Run Free

One really good thing about being retired is the long and winding roads you travel through life become a little straighter, fewer curves and certainly more roadside rests. Since taking a breather I think I have accomplished more than I did during my entire working life. I am not sure that these new accomplishments really matter when I step back and look at the big screen, but I do know that I have become a much better person for having stepped away from the rigors of everyday life.

After more than four decades since I first heard of transcendental meditation there may actually be something to it. Not that I am even sure what that really is I do have time to meditate. Time to review and analyze my mistakes and my winning moments.

To replay challenges posed by others whom for whatever their personal reasons made attempts to derail my goals. "Youth is wasted on the young" is a gross understatement. When we are young we do not understand, nor do we believe that, because the chip in our brain is programmed to think we will never outgrow our youth. That we will beat the odds of nature and never get old.

Stupid phrases like, "You're only as old as you feel" sound pretty good so we make a pact with ourselves that we will always feel young. Or try to think it.

Then one day some young idiot calls you an old man and you start to wonder, "Didn't he get the memo?" I am as young as I feel. Then you realize, no I am not.

Nevertheless, the silver lining is that as we age we know what is going to become of the idiot who called us old. He will be old soon enough and by then we will have already gone through it and it will be his turn.

If I am lucky I will be dead anyway and will not have to deal with him.

A lot of people in my age bracket have probably thought to themselves, "I wish I could be about seventeen years old and know what I know now." If we could do that we would probably all have everything we ever wanted, including better health because we would have taken better care of ourselves.

If we knew then what we know now none of us would have married the wrong person, taken the wrong job, or allowed ourselves to ever be placed in a dangerous situation.

We would have been more careful to elect good leaders and we would have paid more attention to those we have lost and planned better for our futures, maybe established a few customs that would make getting old something to look forward to, something cool.

That is what I meant when I said I have accomplished more and have become a better person since my retirement. Instead of getting out there everyday and competing with those younger and stronger than me, I can watch from the sidelines as they step over each other for a place in line or knock each other down as they climb the social and professional ladders.

Some of those ladders I have already climbed down from. The view up there was not that great. It was not worth what I allowed to slip away to get up there. What I missed by always being on the fast track.

When I think back, and if you have followed my stories, you know I have often, I wonder why I poured so much passion into the things I did. Because in the end, this is just a diary. Scrapbook full of newspaper clippings, photographs, and boxes of tape recordings from hundreds of radio programs. The medals and certificates of appreciation and achievement from law enforcement are just trinkets of my chosen trades. Meaningless stuff. Or is it?

Run Through the Jungle

Every time someone I have known dies, whether I liked them or if I hated their guts, I am reminded of the misnomer of "Whoever dies with the most toys wins."

That person still dies.

These are some of the ways I have become a better person, and why the accomplishment of learning to put things in better perspective is probably my most meaningful achievement. The other stuff is no more than a long obituary. Accounts of how one spent their time on this planet, who they knew-that sort of thing.

Nevertheless, it is here where someone can really know who I am, if they care to. I have had time to analyze and write about some things and some people, including family, friends and foes. Friends come and go so I do not dwell much on where they go or why. Family will be family.

Pretty close to my analogy of friends. I have family members that I barely know because they are busy doing what I used to have to do.

But that's okay because some of them still have to compete with the rest of the world. I leave them to their priorities. It is the foes that I still keep my eye on.

Some never go away, and when some do, others want to take their place. The late Franklin County Sheriff, Earl O. Smith taught me many valuable lessons, none more important than his advice to keep your friends close, but keep your enemies closer. It is easier to control them if you do not lose sight of them. It has been easier to do this since I am not as distracted as I was a few years ago.

So now that I have morphed into this older, wiser former "player" I plan to, as Joe Nuxall said at the end of his broadcasts, round third and head for home. And like I said at the start, it is a straighter line.

However, as I make yet another run at the competition out there, it will be more of a calculated gallop and less of a dash. I have been stuffing my sleeves with new tricks. A lot of what I've picked up along life's complicated journey comes from a friendship I've enjoyed for 30 years with a man who never went to college, never stayed on a job he didn't enjoy and never allowed anyone to dictate his attitude.

He is a veteran of World War II, has been a business man and a con-man (by his own admission) a Bible enthusiasts and a hell raiser (at the same time) he has taken on the legal system acting as his own defense and usually winning and he has owned all the toys. He has played with them and thrown them away when he got bored with them.

His name is Roy Juengel and as he enters his ninth decade on earth he is still laughing at his detractors, staying two steps ahead of a system that is sometimes less than kind to his generation and still wakes up every morning cognizant of the mistakes he has made but satisfied to have learned from them.

I write about Roy Juengel because he is not unlike many who I met during my years in radio. Like some others, I came to know him as a caller to WMNI around 1979. Like me, Roy was going through some difficult emotional times over a woman.

Like a song by Waylon Jennings called "A long time ago" women have been my trouble since I found out they weren't men, in spite of that I stopped and took a wife now and then. That was country music at its finest for guys like Roy and me.

I was working in the perfect spot for a guy going through the trauma of divorce, Roy had already been through it and was figuring out his future as well and I think that was why we connected and formed a bond of friendship that has lasted till now.

In the years that were to pass, I got that divorce and remarried. Not uncommon for radio personalities, and not uncommon for guys like us to seek out others like us if just to know that regardless of our mistakes, or our short comings, life really does mirror the music we hear.

I will never forget the song Roy often wanted to hear on the radio, it was by the Eagles and it was called "Lyin' Eyes." I knew that he could not stand that song and I knew why. I knew many of my listeners the same way. Working at a country music station was like living within the music we played. Songs like "He stopped loving her today" by George Jones almost sent another listener over the edge when I played it for him. The humor in it for me was when he called to ask for it he would say, "Play that one that makes me cry."

Country music, man!

It was like living inside a jukebox at times, living life and playing it on the radio.

Songs never brought tears to my own eyes, but I got these guys. I understood them. I could relate to their anguishes, and I knew how to keep them listening to the radio. I also knew that through the music I played I could attract my own company when I got lonely. Finding affection from the opposite sex was never much of a challenge in those days, anymore than finding another job was. If I needed to be, I could become a chameleon. Moving around from rock and roll to country, to talk radio to legalized gun slinging, speeding on public roadways in a police car, battling drunks and locking up bad guys and then one day walking away from all of it, then reflecting back on it. And knowing that I have something worth writing about.

My candor here about such personal matters explains the title of this book. The title speaks to my view of a life itself and how music was not just a contributing factor in how I made my living for a number of years, but how it helped me to meet and make friends with people who would impact my life in very profound and compelling ways. And as guys like Roy and me speed toward the end of our runs, we can look back, maybe write about and share with others what was important to us and why, and at the same time know that we did what was right.

If just for us.

Take This Job and Shove It

Ohio country music legend, Johnny Paycheck provided one of my more memorable moments as a country music DJ back in 1978. I was working for WMNI and was given the assignment of emceeing Paychecks concert at the Ohio State Fair.

At the time, the big shows were held at the racetrack on the fairgrounds and this one drew what became the largest crowd for a concert in the state fair history.

More than 80,000. It broke a record previously held by Bob Hope.

Emceeing a concert is not that big of a deal, walk out on stage for a previously agreed amount of time, welcome the crowd, introduce yourself and spend a few minutes doing what you hope will be an entertaining monologue. Then introduce the act and walk off to thunderous applause. Easy work for fifty bucks a pop, good money then.

So there I was on perhaps the hottest afternoon of the summer wearing my best Waylon Jennings leather cowboy hat, a white long sleeved shirt and a leather vest, sweating bullets. I did what I was supposed to do out there when I noticed a stagehand off to the side holding a blackboard telling me to stretch; Paycheck was going to be late. I was done with my prepared material and all I could see was the 80 grand stomping their feet all pumped for some country twangin'.

I really do not remember much of what I said after telling them there was a slight delay, but whatever I continued to babble about made the foot stomping more intense. Finally, after what seemed like an eternity I could tell by the crowd's reaction that the star had made his way onto the stage behind me. And as I turned around to welcome him again he tripped over a guitar chord or something else on the stage and stumbled right into me and either spit or threw up.

This pleased the record crowd even more. I had a little puke on the front of my white shirt and try as I might, I could not find the crack in the stage to fall into. It was very humbling. As I left the stage, I could hear the first shout of his signature song, "Take this job and shove it!" I thought, "Amen brother."

Act Naturally

Back in the late 1980's while serving as Public Information Officer for the Franklin County Sheriff's office I received a phone call from Bobby Porto, an Ohio State University student film maker asking if our department would be interested in participating in a comedy film he was producing.

After getting the approval of Sheriff Earl O. Smith, I agreed provided I could include my best friend at the time, Corporal Denny Verbance. Verbance and I worked well on other projects and he was perfect for one of the acting roles we would be involved with.

On the morning of the "shoot" we had arranged to "borrow" the new cruiser that had been delivered to the Major in the patrol bureau, at that time, Major Al Clark.

We were told to take very good care of it. I am not sure the Major had even driven it yet.

The plot to the movie was a guy who had just been released from a hospital following a nervous breakdown would run into all sorts of chaos while riding a bus across town. And in the end he would come face-to-face with a rough neck with a bad attitude that would pull a gun on him only to be stopped by two sheriff's deputy's, myself and Verbance.

The "thug" with the gun was Willie Phoenix, a well-known rock star in the Columbus area who always looked dangerous, acting or otherwise.

The "victim" was played by Larry Ramey of the comedy troupe, "Midwest Tool And Die Company."

Larry and I had previously worked together as DJ's at WMNI back in the '70s. Our role as cops consisted of us pulling up and seeing one man holding a gun on another and bailing out of the cruiser to save the guy. To do this we were required to come screaming down High Street, slam on the brakes and run to his rescue.

Allowing Verbance to drive the cruiser probably was not the best way to do this, but since he was a supervisor and I was not the choice was made. By him.

We probably had to circle the block from Broad Street to High then over to Third Street and back a half dozen times or more to get just the right shot. In addition, we had to do this with lights and siren as we came rolling up to the scene. Denny enjoyed his work that day. And although we did not harm the car, we did "break it in."

Had the Major been there he may have taken away our keys. I know that some tire tread was worn away and I will leave it at that.

We both had speaking roles in the movie and although our lines were brief, it took several takes and retakes to get them out because neither one of us could look at the other without cracking right up. I do not remember if it was because of Denny's driving, or if it was because our lines were really stupid.

And although our lines were very official police type dialogue, Willie's rant was laced with a lot of vulgarity, "Fuck" this, "Fuck" that."

When we went to the screening of the movie, I was surprised at how well it turned out. It was funny and we actually came off believable. Stars, the two of us.

The movie was scheduled to run on public access channel 21 within days of the screening and Sheriff Smith was excited to see it.

I was not very eager to tell him when it would be on because I didn't know how he would react to the "R" rated language in the film. Especially since his name was on the credits when the movie ended.

It might have appeared that he endorsed what we helped make. And I wasn't eager to tell Major Clark because I was not sure how he would respond to seeing his new cruiser being broken in "properly."

After the movie aired on television, I got a call from the Sheriff and the Major.

Although both were good sports about it, both paid homage to my fears. Bobby Porto wanted to meet the sheriff and thank him personally but I found a way to politely explain that the sheriff wanted no thanks. As a matter of fact, I knew better than to try that move myself.

Stormy

Several years ago while working as a third shift patrolman in Obetz, I noticed a known village hell-raiser and his buddy acting strangely in the parking lot of a gas station. By all appearances, both were drunk.

This guy had been a pain in my ass for several months previously, including having had to arrest him for domestic violence and discharging a firearm within city limits.

That last charge would have been comical had it not been such a serious offense.

He claimed he shot at his girl friend as she chased him into his house, after chasing him in her car for several miles. He stated he fired at her because she threatened to "beat his ass" if she caught him. This from a man who claimed to be a former Navy Seal.

But back to the night WCMH television Meteorologist Jym Ganahl helped me nail him for reckless operation of a motor vehicle. I could not make the charge of driving drunk because I did not catch him behind the wheel so I settled for what I could get. He was slick, but not slick enough to get away completely.

After watching these guys play leapfrog in the snow as both sang Christmas carols off key, I watched as they got into their car to leave. Having spotted me, they quickly got out and sat on the hood hoping to wait me out. After about a half hour I pulled my cruiser off the lot and behind an adjacent business figuring that they would think I left. They did and as they peeled out of the gas station, I gave chase.

The weather that night was not conducive for a high-speed car chase but that did not bother them, they blacked out and lost me in a residential area not far from the driver's home. Knowing his address, I proceeded there and sure enough, I found his car crashed into the fence that surrounded his yard. Steam was pouring from under the hood and he had left the headlights on, as well as a blinking turn signal.

I followed the footprints in the snow from his car to his back door and I knocked several times. Naturally, there was no response. So after several minutes of being ignored I went back to my cruiser where I proceeded to write several tickets to be served on him later.

A few days later he came to the police station and filed a police harassment complaint against me. In his complaint he stated that I woke his sick mother when I pounded on his door, and that I lied about his driving dangerously.

In part he stated there was not any ice or snow on the ground so there was no way I could have followed his tracks in the snow as I had written in my report.

After hearing of his complaint against me I sent an e-mail to Jym Ganahl at channel 4 asking if he could provide me with the weather conditions of that particular evening and he wrote back stating that we had received two inches of snow that night. Of course by the time the complaint was filed it had melted.

So armed with Jym's assurance that it did indeed snow at that time I took my "evidence" to our prosecutor who agreed that if anyone would know Jym Ganahl would. With his help I got a conviction, and because of Sergeant Jim Triplett's thorough investigation of the complaint against me I was cleared of any police misconduct. Sometimes things just seem to work out.

Leader of the Pack

In 2003 President Bush came to the Village Of Obetz to speak to workers at a small aluminum plant called "Central Aluminum." As the chief of police I met with members of the United States Secret Service several times in the days leading up to Mr. Bush's visit.

The role our department would play, as well as those of the Columbus Police Department, the Ohio Highway Patrol and the Franklin County Sheriff's Office was discussed. Security planning for the prez was intense.

On the day of his arrival, Obetz had hopped up on the world stage and there were as many media organizations as there were security details in our town. As Mr. Bush went into his long-winded schpeel about nothing I was sitting in the front row paying little attention to what he was talking about, and instead watching the Secret Service agents on the stage on either side of him. Moreover, they were watching me.

Especially one who it seemed never took his eyes off me.

The reason dawned on me. I was in full dress uniform, which meant that I was, sitting about fifteen feet from the most powerful man in the free world with a loaded firearm. Granted there was an army of security personnel stationed strategically throughout the factory, but I began to wonder if this might have been a security breech.

I started thinking; I hope I do not get a cramp that would cause any sudden jerking motion. Or an itch that would cause me to lift my folded hands from my lap. Therefore, I sat there for what seemed an eternity.

Hoping that the president would hasten his visit.

When he did finish most of the "dignitaries" in the front row rushed from their seats to shake his hand and hopefully have their picture taken with him, including those in my party, Obetz Mayor Louise Crabtree and Village Administrator Odis Jones. Odis grabbed me by the arm and said "c'mon, I don't like him either but this is a once in a lifetime chance."

I got up and headed for the exit. Besides, I was only there because my job required me to be. I really did not want my picture taken standing too close to him; I just did not care for him, once in a lifetime moment or not.

Later that day I discussed the ordeal with the agent in charge of co-coordinating the various roles of the "locals" and he laughed. He explained that all of us had been checked out in ways we could never know. And that no one who might have been remotely considered as a security risk would have even gotten near the parking lot let alone inside, sitting that close.

If I am ever in a similar circumstance, I might be tempted to wear a tank top and Bermuda shorts and sit in the back row.

Medicine Man

In the early days of personality radio, not long after big production broadcasting when studios resembled auditoriums to accommodate actors and live musicians, there were some fascinating personalities in our market.

Doctor Bop and Spook Beckman I have already talked a little about. However, there were many others that found their way onto the airwaves here.

Among some of the more colorful characters was Doc Lemon. I was too young to appreciate Doc in his early years, but I came to hear a lot of great stories about him during my time at WMNI. For a guy who had been long gone from that station when I joined up he had more members in his fan club than the rest of us.

Excluding perhaps Ron Barlow.

Everyone it seemed knew the guy personally.

Listeners would actually get mad if I could not tell them "Whatever became of 'Old Doc?" My favorite was "You'll never be another Doc Lemon." Another was, "Ain't been no good DJ on that station since 'Old Doc left."

Working in the shadow of Carl Wendelken, "The Old Nightcrawler" was almost more than I could live up to. I replaced Carl after he left the air to go into the stations promotion department. Listeners did not quit asking, "When's Old Carl comin' back?" For about two years. "Hey! What's wrong with the guy who took his place!!?" Talk about an ego buster.

And they never stopped asking about Doc Lemon.

Especially Mrs. Dotson, a woman who never slept. She was a regular caller day and night. She could not get enough of Elvis Presley. A constant reminder to me that I would never be another Doc Lemon and Carl was the last real country DJ on the station, and all could be forgiven if only I would play more Elvis records.

She once told me if I was trying to fill Carl's shoes I should take them off because they didn't fit!" Carl probably played lots of Elvis records.

It is fun to reflect on the days when I played country and western cowboy records on the electric radio. We were "Country Gentlemen."

The guys who offered a "Tip o' the white stetson" to our businessman of the day, and roses if it happened to be a lady. "The Good Neighbor station." Country, when Country Wasn't Cool.

Hazy Shade of Winter

From time to time I have written about some of the brightest guys in radio and it is probably a given that I admired several of them, and learned something from all of them.

When I went to work for WRFD I was hired by Dave Winters, a laid-back guy who never interfered with what was going on in the studios

I remember showing up about 5:00 Am on a Saturday so he could train me on the equipment and show me how to take transmitter readings and all of the new adventures of learning policies and procedures, and Dave had the studio monitor on mute and had WCOL-FM cranked up. How he could listen to one station while operating another was amazing. Stereo Rock 92 as it was known played hard rock music.

We were easy listening. Dave told me my biggest challenge was to stay awake.

His advise was to keep 'COL-FM on to help do that. I only saw him two or three times during my stint with the station. Moreover, I never received a negative memo or heard anyone say anything negative about him. He was invisible. This helped make working there an absolute panacea.

WRFD was located on a picturesque piece of land at Route 23 and Powell Road, back before they turned all of Delaware County into a zoo.

That corner was actually rural and peaceful. Today it is more like Polaris Parkway on steroids.

We had a lake outside of our studio window to gaze at as we played and listened to smooth music, and for the most part, any song we wanted. Dave did not care. Our play list was almost whatever we wanted it to be. Provided our selections came from whatever records were in the studio. Records, round things with grooves made out of vinyl.

There was something serene about WRFD. The sales staff was laid back, the engineers were forgiving, our news staff was friendly and the jocks all liked each other. I did not know it then but that was a once in a lifetime combination.

And the fact that Spook Beckman was there only added to the good Karma.

Spook was like our grandfather. All of us grew up watching him on television and hearing him on the radio. I was fortunate to work with him twice. As I mentioned several pages ago, we hooked up again at WCOL in the early '80s.

After Winters left and went out into the world, he was replaced by Jim Keyes.

And that too was a good thing. Jim was another guy who liked bending traditional radio rules and allowed us to be creative. If WRFD was considered the Rural Farm Delivery station for Columbus radio, that was okay, because we were relaxed. Without the stress that came with the more powerful ratings leaders. For me working there was an opportunity to stop and smell the radio roses.

Nineteenth Nervous Breakdown

Everyone has experienced first day job jitters and as I continue to reflect on some of the "odd" jobs I picked up along my journey to middle age I have yet another piece of personal trivia.

It was the summer of 1976; I was still with WTVN Radio and a regular spectator at the Columbus Motor Speedway. One of my favorite hangouts since I was about eight years old. I had established a friendship with Bill Ashworth aka Foggy Goggles the previous year. Bill was the track announcer and a sports writer for the Columbus Dispatch. He wrote motor sports stories for the paper and for the speedways program.

At the close of the '75 season Bill approached me to replace him in the tracks announcers' booth the following year. He had suffered a heart attack and retired.

I met with the track owners, the Nuckles family and was given the job. In some ways it was kind of cool sitting up there in the best seat in the house, but it meant a night of working as opposed to an evening of enjoying the action as a spectator.

Prior to taking that job, Sunday nights had been a special time to sit with my family and closest friend on turn four to relax and take in those mouth watering aromas of exhaust, beer and gray hot dogs. After the first night in the booth I knew that I would not be back in 1977.

Somehow, I managed to struggle through the season and when it was over I realized that although I had the best seat in the house, I missed what was happening on the track. A track announcer at a venue like that has no time to cheer his favorite drivers or watch the track officials clean up debris following spectacular crashes.

Between trying to keep up with drivers positions, track speeds, paging visitors to the foot of the tower and announcing winning numbers from the programs, not to mention the chaos that comes from the seven or eight others helping out in the booth. The announcer becomes too busy to spectate. This job paid $50.00 a night and came with first day jitters every night.

When the 1977 season rolled around I was more than happy to hand the chair over to Jerry Beck. The same Jerry Beck who worked for a number of years at what was then known as WLWC-TV-4. Beck was a unique personality. Those who remember the days when the three local TV channels signed off at midnight might remember that it was Jerry who first hosted an overnight program. Saturday nights it was "The All-Night Theatre.

Crummy movies with Jerry's relaxed-I'm-not here attitude. During commercial breaks he demonstrated his usual slapstick corny humor, like stretching a rubber chicken as he would ask, "Wanna see chickie a little longer?" But hey, it was all-night TV. Something new in Columbus.

When he took over the announcing booth duties I found myself again sitting on turn four on Sunday nights. But still unable to pay close attention to the action on the track. I found myself listening to Jerry. He had brought that familiar dry, witty personality to the speedway. He was a true comedian, making fun of the fans, the racecars and everything else that goes along with driving fast, turning left and those who enjoy that sort of thing.

And as I listened I wondered, why didn't I think of that? Beck had turned Sunday nights at the speedway into "The Jerry Beck Show."

One Tin Soldier

Shortly after I took over the all-night show from Carl Wendelken at WMNI back in the late 1970's, I started to meet many of Carl's fans, either while hosting the live country music program broadcasted from the stage of the Southern Theatre, or by having them stop by the studios late at night, or simply on the phone as the insomniacs called in looking for a song or someone to talk to.

Our Country Cavalcade was a local version of WSM's Grand Ole Opry Show, and like the grand daddy of them all, we featured live acts on Saturday nights from a beautiful, historic theatre.

After the programs regular host, Ron Barlow left WMNI, Carl inherited the hosting duties, and later we began taking turns when Carl started getting busier as the stations Public Affairs Director. I actually met my wife at the Cavalcade.

What a groupie.

However, I met another person one night who became obsessed with my radio show because like me, he was a Waylon Jennings fan and I peppered my program nightly with 'Ol Waylon songs. This guy claimed he was the "outlaws" first cousin. And a long-time friend of Carl's, or so he said. He was by today's definition a stalker.

Calling every night on the phone, showing up at WMNI events and eventually waiting for me to get to the studio so he could sit in and watch me do my show.

After turning him away several times by telling him it was against station policy to have visitors in the studio, I arrived one night and he was in the studio.

The DJ on before me, Joe Higman had let him in. Joe said the guy had brought me some homemade chili and some homemade beer to wash it down. So I had a visitor.

He insisted I eat the chili, which I did and felt like I was going to die. It was the hottest food I had ever suffered through. The man had made it with every hot-pepper known to mankind and had laced it with pepper-spray (mace) to give it a kick. The beer was in a clear glass Pepsi bottle and had a gray hue to it and what looked like a combination of sand and flies floating in it.

He said he was seeking a patent on both with the hope of marketing it as a combo deal to be served in bars. But after eating the chili, the beer actually went down pretty smooth. I would have drunk cold piss after that. I'm not sure I did not.

This guy was over six feet tall and weighed way north of 250 pounds. His hair was longer than my shoulder length locks and he had a beard more scraggly than Hank Junior.

As we conversed between the Waylon Jennings records, at least three each hour, I kept hinting to him that he needed to leave because if my boss showed up I could be fired. His response was that if the boss showed up he would kick his ass.

By midway through my show, I learned he was a former POW during the Viet Nam War. He lifted his shirt to expose scars that were hard to look at. He said he got them from "Gooks" who tied him up with barbed wire and hung him from a bamboo tree for hours every day. He told me of other tortures that he endured while living in a warehouse that was only four feet high from floor to ceiling.

For him the war never ended and never would. He claimed that he had killed more Orientals after he was released and sent home than he did in the war. He actually said that he was a serial killer.

Every chance he got, whether it was ambushing someone in a restroom at a dark night-club late at night, to finding them fishing along a river bank and picking them off from long range with a rifle, whenever the opportunity to do it and get away was there. I figured most of what he was telling me was fantasy, another lying storyteller trying to stand taller and seem more important than he was.

Whoever he was, he was creepy, and a little scary considering the present circumstances. Just him and I and a desk clerk down stairs in a seven-story hotel with no security in it.

"Like you" he said to me. "If I had to kill you I'd feel bad for your kids." But if you ever crossed me I'd kill you." Finally he left and I never heard from him again.

I did tell all of this to a Columbus Police officer who would occasionally stop by late at night for a cup of radio station coffee. "Wow" was about all he said.

The Times of Your Life

If life experiences can be compared to the selections on a jukebox, then perhaps the details are in the few photos we keep documenting it.

Describing things vocally, or in print is easy but as the saying goes, a picture is worth a thousand words. The problem is not many of us have nearly enough photos of who we are, where we have been, those we have met or of the experiences we have had.

And for most of us the few photo's that we do have could never visually document every important moment, let alone those that do justice to a few. It would require entire volumes, or very thick portfolio's for each of us to record the entirety of our lives, and not just those silly photo ops such as wedding pictures of brides and grooms shoving cake into each other's faces, or naked babies sitting in bath tubs or puppies gnawing on chew toys.

Through the years I have taken my share of pictures and I have had photo's of myself and my surroundings snapped by others, but in the few photo's of what has been my life up till now there aren't enough to really show it. Even though my own photo collection fills several albums. I have hundreds of photos, including many of everyone I am now or have ever been related to, yet I cannot help but think that the best photo ops were missed. I know I missed such chances every day of my life.

For example, opportunities to catch cute kids (mine) doing memorable things, or chances to photograph my parents doing anything while they were still living.

I have a good collection of both but I know that I would probably trade them all for some that were never taken. Perhaps pictures of the same thing but maybe a minute sooner or one later. Who knows?

Then I think about all of the film I wasted aiming at stupid things, taking pictures of meaningless occurrences such as concerts or sporting events. Some people get all giddy and salivate over such evidence that they "were there" but at the ends of the days that will soon begin ticking down to our last ones, who really gives a shit?

It is like when someone hauls out handfuls of their vacation pictures, or of grand kids you will never know or even see up close. We seem to catch those shots but somehow we miss the opportunities to record the very best moments of our lives.

Think of your best day or a moment in time that could be explained in a handful of photos. It might require thousands of pictures just to find the few that truly captured the importance of it. Think of that day or that moment and take a look at what evidence you do have of it. Is it enough or do you wish there had been more film used to document it, or more attention paid to planning?

I have way too many pictures of other peoples programs, things like going to some sort of show, whether it was in a theatre or in someone's field or on some parking lot. Things that seemed important then but mean nothing now. I have pictures of people, some of them very famous and even some who have autographed them, documentation of who I have met.

I have other photos of people I have either worked with, slept with or have challenged or allied with to either destroy or achieve something through the years.

Most of these pictures mean nothing, especially those of folks I no longer know or care about. I have such photos but not the pictures of my life that were never taken. The photos of many of the subjects in this book for example. I wish I had kept a camera with me more in those days.

My Old School

In other essays I've written about my alma mater, Columbus South High School and a few fellow Bulldogs who wore the Blue and Gray, but I haven't talked much about, nor have I written about an abbreviated detour I made in my senior year to Marion Franklin High School, South's arch rival.

In those days, a rivalry that could sometimes become one of violence existed between the two schools. Especially around the annual football or basketball clashes. South and MF were the local high school equivalent to the Michigan/OSU rivalry. There was nothing friendly between students in either school.

I am not talking just of toilet papering the trees. In my senior year some punks from MF came down to South and spray painted their Red colors all over the cement front entrance to the school and a few Bulldog thugs returned the vandalism the following night by painting a Blue stripe around the entire perimeter of MF's building. Violence in the form of fighting and vandalism were not uncommon following sports events, or anywhere else the two student bodies were likely to congregate.

In my last year of high school, having run into a little mischief at South, I was given the option of being kicked out of school, or to transfer to Marion Franklin.

I was willing to take the first option but my parent's chose the latter for me.

So off to Koebel Road I went. I knew my tenure there would be brief, and I did worry that when my new classmates discovered from where I came that life at school could get interesting.

I learned when I got there the differences between the two schools was more striking than I tried to imagine. Marion was a predominately-white populated school with only a few hundred black students among its 1200-plus student body.

South on the other hand was something closer to a 60/40 split among the nearly 3000 black and white students who went there and we did not always accept one another.

Where South also had a number of longhaired hippie types like myself, the guys at Marion were for the most part clean cut. Some were still squirting Brylcream into their palms and slicking back their hair. Many of these guys looked like they were lost in the 50's.

As fate had it, I met another South transplant who like me wore his hair long and resembled Dennis Hopper in the Movie "Easy Rider." Chuck Wears, a guy who I wish knew longer.

I could not wait to return to South, back to where I felt at home among the muggers, thugs and thieves. And like many other poor choices I made in my youth,

I soon regretted going back. When Chuck Wears told me that I would like Marion I thought he was nuts. I guess I was too busy trying to connive my way back into South to see that he had been right all along. However, during my first few days back there I understood what he was talking about.

Marion Franklin hatred for all things Blue and Gray was born out of retaliation for how they were treated by South students dating back several years before I got caught up in the rivalry. (According to my Red Devil pals.)

I had more altercations with Bulldogs I knew most of my life than I ever would have had at MF.

The *education* I was getting from the Columbus Public School system was nowhere near as valuable as the lessons I got in the study of human behavior.

The rivalries that still exist between those schools have is still there.

Now they settle issues with weapons instead of fists. Nevertheless, in spite of these mixed emotions, now when I hunt the scores of high school football and basketball games, I find myself hoping to see both in the winner's column. And when they meet each other, I am never disappointed, regardless of the outcome. Because either way, my school wins.

Cowboys to Girls

Before the mid 1960's the Schmidt's Packing Company located at the corner of East Kossuth Street and Jaeger Street had been a Southside landmark for decades.

I was thinking about the days when I was a kid and some of us would hang around and watch the delivery of animals to be slaughtered there and fantasizing way's to set them all free and spare them from the butchers inside. I could not help but to feel sorry for them especially when I saw the Schmidt's employees milling around with blood soaked White coats. Slaughterhouses still depress me when I think of them.

My Dad worked at one at Lockbourne Road and Frebis Avenue called Swifts Premium Meats and I used to hate the stories he told of how the cattle were barbarically slaughtered there. He liked telling those stories at the dinner table to aggravate my mother.

At 15, I joined my best friend Danny Sauer working at Schmidt's, but by this time the packing plant had been torn down and the business moved across the street into an old stable and became known as Schmidt's Sausage Haus.

We were among the first employees of the restaurant when it opened in the summer of 1967. Located just two blocks down the street from my home the commute was the only easy part of that wake up call for both of us to the working world. Going into my sophomore year at

South High School was probably the year that I actually morphed from a kid to an adult, partly because of that job, but mostly because of the year ahead.

In this sense Danny and I grew up together, even though we only knew each other since 1964 and by our senior year in high school would drift apart. It is odd sometimes when I remember what seemed important to Danny and me during those years.

Hormones had something to do with our zeal to earn as much money as we could because we were both egotistical enough to think we would go into high school as the most prolific of all girl chasers and owners of the coolest cars in the South end.

Giving up our paper routes and going to work at Schmidt's for $1.00 an hour gave us an edge because even though we were students that had to be in school at 8:15 in the morning, we worked from 4:00 PM until midnight most days and after taxes would earn something like $35.00 a week.

High cotton for the times. Danny and I were as good of friends as anyone could be. We seemed glued together.

Getting up at 7:00 each morning for school wasn't the easiest thing either of us did because in addition to working late on school nights we would walk about a block going home and stopping across the street from the old packing plant and talking. We would stand on the corner just chatting as if neither one of us was ready to call it a night and go home.

Sometimes we would hang around on the corner for an hour or more, and occasionally drawing the attention of a passing cop wondering what we were up to.

My parents might have thought we were running the streets after work and getting into trouble, but they knew that Dan was the least likely person to do anything outside the law. I knew it too and that had a lot to do with why we were friends.

I can not imagine that in any of those discussions was any talk of what our neighborhood would be in the future, how it would become the ritzy area it now is and because of the money that has flowed into the Village has caused it to become a target for the worst of criminals.

I doubt that we could have imagined that if we came back at midnight sometime in 2008 and stood on that corner we might be mugged or shot.

German Village was a quiet area in those days and thoughts of robberies and shootings could not be further from our minds. Instead, we were thinking and discussing girls and our dream cars.

For me it was a 1960 Ford Falcon and for Danny a 1963 Chevy ll. Our first cars when we turned 16. I would like to look him up someday and take another walk around the area, maybe stop at the corner of East Kossuth Street and Jaeger and see if his memory is as good as mine. Because when I think back on those days I remember that just walking around at night, talking and making plans for our futures was what we did most of the time before we got those jobs at Schmidt's.

There were nights we probably walked for miles, regardless of the weather. In addition, when I think about all of that it becomes clear to me that that is how friendships are built and how they survive. Spending great deals of time talking.

By the time Danny Sauer and I stopped being friends there really was no reason to stop knowing him. No fallouts, nothing that would cause two best friends to drift apart.

In the years since we left high school we have spoken to each other only a few times, even though we still live within ten miles of each other. I guess we just ran out of things to talk about.

The Wurlitzer Prize

With the ease and availability of "free" or almost free music now, we are getting further away from the times when people were willing to drop coins into a jukebox to hear their favorite songs.

With so many devices available now to carry ones entire music library with them everywhere they go, what are the percentages that anyone could make a living servicing table top music machines or those behemoth floor models that used to dot almost all eateries and taverns?

The Crosley-Select-O-Matic and Seaburg table models are still around in some retro themed diners and the big Wurlitzers still lurk in many taverns, but I wouldn't think they rake in the change they did a few decades ago.

I can recall the days when a favorite song would cost a dime to hear and three favorites would cost an entire quarter. Expensive when you consider the many web sites one can go to get free tunes to download into their I-Pods or telephones.

This could be a good thing for those of us who remember sitting somewhere hearing another persons thirst to hear their crappy taste in music, or someone who just couldn't get enough of one song that they would play over and over.

I really do not miss trying to eat and hearing a jukebox blasting Kitty Wells when I might have been in the mood for Deep Purple music. I remember leaving a place once because some guy kept playing "Daddy Don't You Walk So Fast" by Wayne Newton.

One could only assume that he might have been feeling guilt pangs over walking out on his family. The song would come on, he would bury his face in his hands and weep, then when the song was over he would play it again, and again. It was horrible.

I did not feel sorry for that sap, I wanted to attack him.

One reason that I love almost everything Three Dog Night recorded except "Joy to the World" is because one could not walk into a campus bar in 1971 without hearing it. Over and over.

Jeremiah was a bullfrog? Please.

Other tunes that became annoying thanks largely to jukebox over play were "Hang On Sloopy" and "Louie, Louie." Cool when they first came out but soon relegated to ear splitters with over saturated play.

Oldies radio stations still beat them to death.

But no song, not even "99 Bottles Of Beer On The Wall" played in its entirety, or "Achey Breaky Heart" makes me gag anymore than "Unchained Melody" by the Righteous Brothers. That song sucks; it cannot be disputed by anyone so go away.

Nauseating when it first came out, critically sickening when it became a favorite on dance floors and terminal after radio station program directors watched the movie, "Ghosts."

When I was working at WCOL listeners to my show knew not to call and request that one, and those who did ask for it waited for long periods for nothing. Even our Program Director, Michael Cruise was hip to the fact that I would not play that song even if it meant risking being fired.

And he was one of those PD's who spent a great deal of time chastising me for not sticking to the crappy play list that was left in the studio for me to follow. Cruise and I rarely saw eye-to-eye, and almost never agreed on what constitutes good music. One of those programmers who didn't seem to believe that The Rolling Stones recorded anything besides "Can't Get No Satisfaction" or that Steppenwolf made better songs than "Born To Be Wild."

However, he seemed to love "Unchained Melody." That thing was programmed it seemed every hour on the hour. I would have rather played Al Jolson records on the wrong speed. As a matter of fact, a duo of Jolson and Rudy Valley singing "Achey Breaky Heart" through megaphones would have gotten more air play on my show had they recorded such a disaster.

As I have written often, my musical taste is all over the super highway. Various moods will have me listening to anything from Head Banging Rock & Roll to Bubble Gum to Do Wap, or Sinatra to Boxcar Willy to Slim Whitman.

Rarely will I sit through anything categorized as a love song, but once in awhile I can stomach a bit of it. The defining phrase in that previous statement is one's perception of once in awhile. More than once a month gets annoying.

My spouse likes music by Barbra Striesand. When I hear her music, I have to pop four Excedrins and retreat to a dark, quiet room.

Just My Imagination

Writing about broadcasting and the small part I played in it as a radio announcer for nearly twenty years comes easy to me because I've never grown tired of thinking back and remembering some of the most fascinating people I've met through the years. Those I grew up listening to, some I had the chance to work with and of course many who I met as listeners, some of whom had a profound effect on my life.

Unlike the visual media, radio forced listeners to use their imagination.

The voice coming out of the speaker could have been put with any face a listener wanted to match it with. In the early days of radio dramas the same was true for whatever was being described.

I can remember lying in bed listening to a transistor radio, sometimes very late at night, listening for my favorite Top-40 songs, but willing to hear a program on WCOL that aired each day around 2:30 AM called "Unshackled".

The program was a half hour long drama that must have been programmed to satisfy some Federal Communications Commission requirement to air a required amount of public service programming.

It was a religious show that featured various actors playing out roles of someone down trodden, hopelessly lost and with him or her in the end finding someone to point them to Jesus. The show was actually very well done and was complete with sound effects that included real street sounds such as vehicles driving by, footsteps, wind, thunder and rain and through the wonder of dubbing and over dubbing actually sounded very real.

The heavy creaking of a door, glass breaking, dogs barking, all lent to the believability that what was coming out of the radio was very real. The program could leave the listener with a visual of something like an old drunk lying on the steps of a mission as a Police Officer walking the beat stops and threatens to arrest him for vagrancy only to have someone come out of the church offering to take him in.

Once inside the vagrant would be given a blanket to wrap up in, given something warm to drink and then proceed to tell of his hard luck. The person taking him in would listen patiently and then have all the answers to make things right of course.

I have never been accused of being a religious person, not then and certainly not now, so the meaning of this program was lost on me. However, every time I listened to it, I found myself caught up in the story line and feeling sorry for the poor, lost subject of the program. In the end, he or she was always saved from further personal disaster and misery, but the story line carried through to near the end leaving the possibility of a different outcome.

By 3:00 AM when the rock music returned I was usually too tired to keep listening and turned off the radio hoping I never ended up like the person wandering about with little hope and needing rescued in the "Unshackled" story.

I am not old enough to remember radio shows like "The Shadow" and some of the other serials that people had before television. Nevertheless, I can well imagine those before me gathering around the radio caught up in the stories. I do know that sort of entertainment can be addictive.

In the late 1970's while working at WMNI, the station signed up for a program called "CBS Radio Mystery Theatre." It was an hour long program not unlike "Unshackled" except that instead of having story lines of faith and good will, the shows were action dramas, murder mysteries, and each nightly installment was an hour long and the listener had to tune in every night to keep up with the plot.

This was great for me because it aired in the hour before my show so I could listen as I prepared whatever needed prepared for my own program. The only problem was that the last hour of the continued saga aired on Friday nights, my only night off. And by Friday I was so caught up and needing to know how it ended I would find myself at home listening to WMNI to hear the conclusion.

As I said, that sort of programming can be addictive. I can only imagine how much so in the days when that was all there was.

On The Outside Looking In

One of my favorite stories from Larry Roberts, concerns his father and the early days of television, Larry's father owned one of the first television stores in Chillicothe back in 1949 when the medium was still new and he would leave one turned on in the window after hours for passer-by's to see, even rigging an outside speaker so viewers could hear what they were watching.

Some would bring lawn chairs and sit on the sidewalk to marvel at it.

It is funny how when we look back on things like this we can some times relate and say to ourselves, "I did that too." What Mr. Roberts was doing in Ross County was being done on East Whittier Street here on the south side of Columbus at a small electronics' store called Buckeye Radio Lab when I was a kid in the early 1960's.

Although by 1961 and 62 most people had television sets in their homes, few in this area had color sets. In fact, I did not know anyone who owned one and we did not get our first color TV until 1964. Color television was something just a little short of amazing in those days and the programs broadcasted in "Living Color" were few and far between.

Stations would announce at the beginning of programs the fact much like today when they make a big deal if it is in High Definition.

HDTV is nothing compared to the phenomenon that color television was in its infancy.

So to experience the thrill of it, some of us would trickle over to Buckeye Radio Lab and stand on the sidewalk, sometimes in the cold and watch programs that we would not otherwise bother with but to see them in color.

One morning my fascination and appreciation of the sets left on in the window there got me in trouble at school. I was in the fifth grade at Siebert Elementary School and I was a patrol boy assigned to that corner. My responsibility was to hold other kids back from crossing until the street was clear of traffic and then hold out my flag to signal safe passage.

I had leaned my flagpole against the side of the building and walked over to see something on television and when I turned around, a woman; probably someone's   mother was using my flag to help kids cross the street. The incident was reported to the school and as a reprimand I was reassigned to a less busy corner. Nevertheless, this story has a happy ending.

After performing so well on a corner that might have seen just two or three cars during my shift I was promoted to the rank of Sergeant. That equated to doing nothing but walking the district to check up on and tell on the other patrol boys if they were caught goofing off.

Within a month of that promotion I was elevated to the rank of Lieutenant when ours withdrew from school and moved away. To be in the right place at the right time!   Like standing on the corner of East Whittier and Bruck Street in 1962 watching the wonders of color television.

Signs

Writing about back then as my son Todd calls the era when I was small, is akin to leafing through old photo albums that exist only in memory. Sometimes when I am trying to describe a certain person, place or event from years back it is like dreaming in black & white.

I can recreate mentally what I am writing about; moreover my minds eye often sees it as if it were newspaper clippings or old television images before the days of color media.

Most of my family's old photographs are black & white prints so maybe a lot of my memory is derived from that. But even without different colorful hue's to see against that flat screen in my head my memory still seems good. And not everything is colorless up there.

In another story I wrote about playing touch football with the neighborhood kids in the old Big Bear parking lot on East Whittier Street back in the early and mid 1960's. When I think back to that activity I am seeing the games in black and white images but when I think of the surroundings I do remember the color. Like the store itself.

Its facade was a pale cream color with large red neon letters spelling out "Big Bear" above a bank of huge glass windows, and at the edge of the parking lot in front of the store stood a mammoth sign with the same neon lighting and a huge outline of a big brown bear also trimmed in red neon lights. At night it illuminated the entire parking lot.

However, what really made that sign special was the large chrome hole in the center of it, big enough for even an adult to climb in and lie down to resemble a human "u". The sign was a south side icon for years. It was also something of another playground for the neighborhood.

Few, if any kids who grew up in this area did not play on that thing, or use it for shelter in bad weather. Tag, "Simon Says" or a game that might have only been known in this area called "1-2-3 Red Light" was common, but so was acting out our favorite movies about war, mountain climbing or pirate ships, whatever we could imagine that sign to be.

It was a vessel with numerous possibilities because its cement base that was elevated a few feet off the ground was like a concrete balcony that encircled the entire structure. The body of it was made of the same pale yellow porcelain as the front of the store.

Rumors that some of us didn't quite comprehend in the early 60's suggested that it was also used as a "back seat" from time to time. By the time I was old enough to fornicate on it-it was gone.

Sometimes Good Guys
Don't Wear White

I met Franklin County Sheriff Earl Smith in the summer of 1986. I really didn't want to meet the man because quite frankly I was intimidated by his fiery, sometimes explosive personality. I had read a lot about him in the papers and seen him in various television interviews enough times to convince me that this was not someone I wanted sitting across a desk from me.

At the time I hosted an afternoon talk radio show on WCOL. It was common to have strong personalities like Earl on my program, but I was in no hurry to have him booked as a guest.

I was used to interviewing people like U.S. Senator John Glenn, U.S. Congressman Chalmers Wylie, Columbus Mayor Dana "Buck" Rinehart and other local politicians, but Earl had a stigma attached to him as a sort of wild-west gunslinger. A tough guy.

I had heard that he was a chain smoking, in your face lawman who would kick your ass first and ask your name later. So when my producer, Todd Rifner came to me one day and informed me that he had booked the sheriff to be a guest on my show, I protested vigorously. I went to our program director at the time, Kevin Young and asked if he could get a fill-in host. I did not want to banter with Earl Smith.

Kevin assured me that it would be fun because Earl was great for generating audience participation. The sheriff had been a guest on every talk show in town but mine, so it seemed to be the right thing to do.

When he showed up that afternoon, I had already warned my board-op in the control room to keep his finger glued to his bleep button. A friend of mine at another radio station had told me that Earl liked to lace profanity into his dialogues. "He might call the county commissioners a bunch of mother f---kers" my friend warned. Great.

So there I sat across from this guy and we began to discuss such issues as why he bought a tank for the sheriff's department to combat crime, why he called the president of the Fraternal Order of Police an ass-hole, why he defied judges by releasing misdemeanor offenders against their orders, why he threatened to lock the judges out of their chambers if they messed with him, the simple everyday headlines surrounding the sheriff's office.

Soon I learned that Kevin Young was right. We could not keep up with the phone calls. And as he carefully and politely explained each criticism, I began to think that he was either a good con man, or everything I had heard about him had been either fabricated or blown out of proportion. The guy was smooth. Tough, but very articulate, patient and likeable.

What was supposed to be a one-hour interview ended up being four. He was that good. Interest in what he had to say was that high. And at the end of the day I asked him if he would come back.

The second time Earl was a guest on my program I asked him how and why he became a lawman. I am not sure I got an answer because he was very good at redirecting the conversation. Soon I realized that he was interviewing me.

He asked how I got into broadcasting, if I liked it, if I ever thought about doing something else, like possibly coming to work for him. He went on to explain that people often misunderstood him, (What?) That sometimes the media tried to exploit his explosive personality and that too often he was portrayed as a bull-headed tyrant. (No!)

Anyway, he was going to create the position of Public Information Officer and he wanted to fill it with someone who could navigate in and around the media. Someone to explain him and the workings of his department. The sheriff's spokesman.

He told me that he liked me and a guy at WTVN and he invited me to submit a resume. At the time I was not ready for a career change because I truly loved broadcasting. However, within days rumors began to circulate that WCOL was being sold and that the new owners were going to heave-ho the talk format and automate the station and get rid of everyone.

With that little morsel of fear planted in my conniving head I called the sheriff and asked if he was still looking for someone to handle his media affairs. He told me that he was and that he was still interested in me and the guy from WTVN. When

I told him that guy had called him a Black-Shirted Gestapo on the air the other night he offered me the job. It was the best I could do, I wanted that job.

The next seven years were not easy. I learned that the sheriff had some vicious enemies. People inside the law enforcement and political communities, some dangerous outlaws-some with healthy bankrolls, certain media people and several special interest groups who would have liked nothing better than to control the sheriff's office.

Some of his worst enemies worked in his own department, some worse than them were members of his political party- Republicans. By the end of his first term in office, his own Republican Party became his biggest detractors. And there I was smack dab in the middle of something I understood, but making others get it was nearly impossible.

One former reporter even published a book about the Smith administration called "Tin Star Tyrant." In it was every shady event that surrounded everyone who was loyal to the sheriff. The book was released within weeks of the election of course.

I found being in the middle of those waging all out war against this man a pretty thankless place to be. Some of the people out to destroy the sheriff were people that I knew and considered friends. I hated what they were trying to accomplish but I understand some of the gripes. Many of the attacks were baseless, and some had credence. However, most of the sheriff's headaches were not of his own doing.

Often times it could be attributed to those he surrounded himself with.

Some of the real power players in the sheriff's office were shady dudes.

Earl O. Smith was not a bad man but he did have a few bad men around him.

He made some mistakes but in many cases, it was my opinion that he allowed himself to be manipulated. Not because he was stupid, but because he trusted the wrong people. Moreover, I told him that many times. So did many others.

If I could sum up what I think his problem was I would say that he was too stubborn for his own good. It eventually cost him an election. That and a few bad apples in high positions within his administration of course.

When Earl Smith passed away, I lost a mentor and a friend. And as tough as that job was, it will always be the most interesting seven years I ever worked. I am glad I told the sheriff that a guy at WTVN compared him to a Nazi. Otherwise, I would not have detoured into a fascinating career.

And I would not have had all of those years to study and get to know one of the most interesting people ever elected to public office in Franklin County.

The Boxer

Those who don't know him won't know his name but may appreciate this short tale anyway about a former deputy sheriff who was liked and admired by most of us who did.

Those who do know him would know who this page is about even if I did not offer as much as a first name here. George who was a deputy sheriff bigger than most men and now among the rank's of us who have retired and have left the dirty work for other's was an absolute joy to work with.

If ever dealing with a big tough guy there were few men I would rather have with me and on my side than him. George was as big as most of them and way more fearless than most men on either side of the law.

When I first met him he was working downtown in the main jail and those guy's never knew who or what sort of person would be brought in but they always knew there would be drama. Like the night when another deputy arrested the heavy weight-boxing champion of the world James "Buster" Douglas for driving while intoxicated.

The tale of George vs. the champ has been told so often it has become something of Franklin County folk lore, and it is one that will be told for years to come, especially by those who were there to enjoy it. I was not there so I cannot vouch for the accuracy but I have absolutely no reason to think any part of it is fabricated.

I did not know anything about it until I showed up for work that morning and found a flood of reporters waiting outside my office- NBC, CBS, CNN, ABC, several newspapers from around the country and of course ESPN were well represented.

All wanting interviews and mug shots.

When the boxing champion of the world gets arrested, it is a major media brawl.

None got to speak to him because his stay with us was brief; millionaires always seemed to be able to bond out quickly. Nevertheless, they did get the mug shots, minus the "bling" the boxer was wearing when he was brought in. I will get to that soon.

I mentioned that when working with George all of us knew we were in capable hands, he was fearless and could back up anything he promised. But I can't say that I was never worried because riding shotgun in a police car driven by him was sometimes a test of not only one's dedication to service and protection, but of the strength and discipline of ones bladder.

Police cars generally have more than enough engine to get down the road in something of a blink if cop's are needed somewhere in a hurry. Some cop cars have enough engine to win at drag strips if the cop it is assigned to is mechanically inclined and is willing to *tune it up a little.*

Moreover, every cop I ever knew appreciated that fact so much that they rarely wanted to waste any of the vehicles performance perks. Is that to say that most cops sometimes drive like maniacs?

Of course it is. Those who swear they have *never* skirted the traffic laws while on duty is either lying or they are not being truthful. Pick one. Is it right? Of course it's not, but many if not all do it and I would challenge any cop who claims to have never pushed his patrol car to the boundaries of capability to say that with a straight face.

That is why I hated riding shotgun with anyone. If I was not controlling it I always worried that my will was up to date and that I left it at home in a place it could be easily found. Back to the opening bell at the Franklin County Jail.

As what has become a hallmark of jail tales has it, the boxing champ was led to the slating counter to be booked on a drunken driving charge and was in no mood to be friendly.

When told to remove his jewelry he balked, backing up as if to challenge anyone to try to take it from him. The supervisor on duty sized him up and then ordered George to remove it for him. As he approached the champ he stated, "You might be the heavy weight champion out there, but I'm the heavy weight champ in here, I've had 3000 fights and I'm 3000 and "0" so give it up."

Douglas removed his hardware and handed it to George. It is a great tale especially if it is all true.

Another great tale would be how George used to describe a particular body appendage of his. He liked to say that it resembled a baby's arm. I once asked if he meant fetus or new born, he replied, "toddler."

Having watched him work, he may have been telling the truth.

Born To Run

In 1991, I traveled to Washington, D.C. to appear on the FOX television show, "America's Most Wanted" and while there, I had the opportunity to hang out with two agents from the Federal Bureau of Investigation.

On the Friday morning before going to the television station for the show, I was accompanied by these guys on a tour of the FBI's Washington Bureau. I would come to rely on them later for investigations here.

Having had the opportunity to experience all that I did during that trip I now realize how special it all was. In these days of "done working" there is more time for personal reflection.

The trip itself came after several days of filming the re-enactment here in Columbus of a segment featuring the escape of Timothy Brewster from Franklin County deputies that year. Brewster was wanted in addition to escape charges for rape and kidnapping.

Happily, he was apprehended two weeks after the airing of the program.

Flying to and from the nations capitol on AMW's dime and being put up in one of D.C.'s finest hotels was special in and of itself, but being chaperoned around town by a pretty blond (Alyson Camerotta) from the FOX network staff was more than I could have begged for and received.

Feasting in high-end restaurants during my stay, a visit to the White House, meeting and talking with John Walsh, "casual" activity in a Chevy Chase, Maryland nightclub, the FBI and U.S. Treasury tours and an abbreviated visit to the Smithsonian Institute made me dislike Tim Brewster a little less for a few days.

Not that I was glad he was AWOL, but not unhappy that "America's Most Wanted" offered their help to catch him. I will get into his story later.

Looking back at 1991 and some of the experiences that came with being Sheriff Earl O. Smith's Public Information Officer I realize how fortunate I really was to have had what now seems like a privilege.

It is funny but at the time, I never saw it that way. At the time, it all seemed like work, even the "perky" type assignments like traveling to other destinations, sometimes for training and other times like the D.C. trip. And, looking back, I have come to accept that era as the end of my youth.

Although I was in my mid 30's I was still taking life a day earlier than it was because I never envisioned how fast it would all go by, or when it did that it would all be gone. Never could I have imagined myself unable to do any job of any kind back then.

Now here I am, in dire need of new energizer batteries. The trip I took in '91 and the pace I kept during it would now be something a little more "ambitious" today.

Being retired and the reasons I am so bring into clear perspective that my early years in law enforcement was more special than I could ever articulate completely.

The Load Out

The most exciting moments of working third shift patrol for me was after roll call when the second order of business was loading the cruiser with the tools and utensils needed for a tour of duty.

Customarily that meant at least enough paperwork, ie; various report forms and packets to last through the night, something called a "posse box" made of aluminum to hold it, a flash-light with a car charger, a shotgun, appropriate element wear such as rain gear or a coat if needed, a plastic tub containing items like extra ink pens, gloves, extra hand cuffs, tape recorder, camera, extra ammo clips, law books, personal hygiene kit, air freshener, packs of cigarettes and a jar of instant coffee.

Then doing the cruiser equipment check, blasting the various siren modes to ensure they worked, as well as the emergency lights such as the light bar on top and various strobes built into neat places like the headlights, tail-lights and rear interior shelf.

Doing the vehicle inspection to make sure I would not be charged with any new dents, dings or paint scratches that might have happened when the officer before me had the car.

And finally, marking in service to let the dispatcher know that wherever I was headed the world around me would become a safer place because in my heart of hearts I knew that I was the most profound and capable cop on the streets. And probably the smartest, most daring and man-of-no-fear out there.

That was me. I guess I should throw in good looking, witty and a little more charming than what was allowed by law as well, I mean, why hold back? Sound like anyone you know? If you know a cop, it probably does.

The reason I say the beginning of the shift was the most exciting part of the day for me was all of the reasons above and because when I keyed up that mike it was with anticipation that the person answering me might have the biggest caper of my career waiting to tell me.

One never knew. If nothing was holding and needing police attention I was free to either go look for my own trouble or drive aimlessly waiting for something to either happen in front of me or for a dispatch.

Before I marked in there was always that hope that the night would start off with something interesting, like starting for a location where someone was beating the hell out of another, or shots fired in an area, or to back up another officer on something interesting and the best of the best for me, a burglary in progress.

Any of the above were good adrenalin accelerators.

A lot of Police work sucks, like standing in traffic directing it, more if its freezing cold or sweltering hot, or filling out paperwork, or sitting in classrooms for in-service training, or being bitched out by superiors and or disrespectful civilians, sitting in emergency rooms with either victims of crimes or with the thugs who need medical attention before being taken to jail.

All of it sucks if working third shift after being awake all day because of court cases, special duty jobs too much fun doing other things or just plain insomnia. Staying awake when the police radio is dead was sometimes more challenging than any actual police work.

There were a few times when I may have not been fully awake. There were times I found other officers in my hiding spots who were sound asleep.

One morning in Obetz, I discovered a fellow officer who I was not particularly fond of asleep in his cruiser while it was parked where I planned to rest. It was around 3:00AM and it was frigid. The area was behind the Columbus Motor Speedway back in a grassy area that was hidden by trees from anyone not familiar with that location.

I pulled my cruiser alongside his and I noticed that his head was tilted back in the seat and his mouth was wide open and when I opened his car door, I heard the most God-awful snore I ever heard. He was completely out.

For a moment, I thought about dropping something down his gullet, perhaps flicking a cigarette ash into his mouth or something tasteless like a small chunk of ice or my finger. Had it been a warmer night, maybe a lightning bug. Instead, I just left his door open thinking the cold air might wake him and got back into my car and waited.

I was hoping he would wake up and know that I caught him sleeping, if for no other reason than he had my spot or just to embarrass him.

The cold air was not doing what I hoped. So I aimed my spotlight at his face and turned it on. After a minute or so, it was clear that this guy slept like a dead man.

I decided to get out and open all four doors of his cruiser and when I did I reached into his car and changed his heater to maximum air conditioning and turned the fan to high, then I turned on all of his emergency flashing lights, including his top beacons, take-down lights and side spot light which I aimed straight toward the sky.

I even turned on his left turn signal and turned his steering wheel all the way to the right and set his emergency brake, and as a final touch I pulled the latch and opened the cars hood, opened his glove compartment and the trunk. Then I drove away.

When I got a few miles down the road I picked up my radio mike and asked the dispatcher to mark him and have him meet me several miles away on the other side of town. When he did not answer, the dispatcher became concerned and marked for any car in the area to be on the lookout for him and to check his well-being.

I would like to say that it took awhile to find him and that when he was found it was by either a supervisor from our department or one from another agency but instead he woke up and heard the call.

After telling the dispatcher that he was okay she advised him to meet with me at a distant location from where he was. I gave him enough time to almost get there and then I cancelled him. It was the right thing to do, I wasn't there anyway.

I was back behind the speedway. Not to sleep, but to rest my weary sense of humor and wish that I could have been there to see his face when he woke up.

The guy was strange, he never mentioned to anyone that he woke up and found all of his lights on, his doors opened and a cold blast in his face from not only the outside air but coming from the vents inside as well. He couldn't have had a clue as to who did all of that and I guess he figured that if he didn't speak to anyone about it no one would be the wiser.

Every cop in zone four was wise. Word got out somehow. I have wondered for years what that officer might have thought when he woke up. Did he suspect me?

Did he even think that it was a cop who messed with him?

My hope is that he woke up and thought that a bunch of kids or some other group of troublemakers did him. I wonder if he checked to see if he still had his wallet. If I knew these things, I would feel better about my actions.

Ups And Downs

Much of what I have shared is documented within the pages of my scrapbooks, comprised mostly of news clippings about murders, vehicle crashes, including cars, trucks, motorcycles and even a few airplanes and one helicopter.

As the public Information Officer for the Franklin County Sheriff's Office for a number of years I was summoned to one ugly place after another to gather releasable facts and assimilate them to the news media.

Seeing body parts strewn through tree's from a plane crash near Port Columbus International to a head embedded into a truck axle as the result of a motorcycle crash were just a few of the horrific things I photographed.

A severed arm from a guy who rolled his pick-up down a hill, something that when I picked it up and laid it on a gurney all I could think about was that it was heavier than it looked, and an ax still left in a young woman's head after she had been executed and a man beaten severely and found impaled on a fence post are a few more.

Early in my law enforcement career there was a teenage girl who had been murdered, wrapped in plastic and found floating in a creek in the village of Valley View and another teenage girl who had multiple stab wounds found in a ditch in Obetz.

Nothing was more unsettling than actually watching a woman burn to death after her compact car exploded in a head-on crash with a truck. Seeing her on fire and thrashing inside of a car that no one could approach because of the searing heat was one of those helpless moments that one never forgets.

When the fire was out and she was pulled from the wreckage her shoes with her feet still in them were melted against the floor and some of her blond hair and part of her scalp hung from what was left of the vehicles headliner.

But what left a more haunting impression was seeing a four year old boy who had been crushed by the family mini-van when it rolled over several times, ejecting him and trapping him beneath the vehicle until it was lifted by a tow truck. That was just a few days before Christmas several years ago and the recovery was witnessed by his young brothers and sisters and their mother who all made it through the crash okay.

From kidnapped kids to victims of abuse what happened to them was never easy to explain. Neither were the suicides, including a few jumpers from bridges, one whose body wasn't retrieved from the Scioto River until it was recovered several weeks later bloated up twice its normal size and missing pieces of flesh and digits that the coroner said were probably eaten away by river life.

Maybe the most vulgar case involved a perverted pathologist working in the Franklin County Coroners Office. This guy photographed himself having sex with corpses, among them a man who had been cut in half when a train rolled over him. He was found out when an alert film developer from a Photomat where he dropped off his film saw the pictures and notified the sheriff's office.

He was charged only with abuse of a corpse, a misdemeanor, although his medical license was revoked in Ohio it was found out several months later that he obtained one in another state.

Accidental deaths besides crashes and fires included two men who fell more than one hundred feet off of oil tankers while working on them on West Broad Street, industrial accidents where either something exploded or someone inhaled deadly gasses, a child who fell off of his father's tractor while being taken for a ride, a man who's tractor rolled over him while mowing on a grade and a kid thrown from his four wheeler head first into a fence post.

I considered writing about each incident individually, but to detail each story, even if only tersely as I have with a few of them in this book would have made this project more than it is intended to be.

I would need help. In my scrapbooks I have kept the clippings of no less than 300 from the newspapers who were interested in what I had to say to them, and of those only a handful involved actual public relations which is what I was originally hired to push the media to cover.

My job became one of one tragedy after another, but there were some brighter moments. Like working with the SWAT team to deliver turkeys to needy families on Thanksgiving, and again with them to haul toys from a radio station to a church for distribution to similarly poor kids. Or, liaison for the Madison Township Athletic Association and a T-Ball team in it sponsored by our office.

There were the fairs and festivals where we erected tents to show off who we were as a department, prime special duty jobs like working OSU basketball games at St. John Arena and at the Columbus Motor Speedway.

Having said that, there were the not so fun special duty gigs like directing traffic for up to ten hours straight in sub zero weather in the winter and when it was in the 90's in July for hours and hours.

One special duty job I was sorry to volunteer for was baby-sitting a farmer's field when a plane crashed into it in the middle of the night. It was so foggy that night that I almost didn't find my way into the field where the craft laid waiting for the FAA guy's who wouldn't be able to investigate it till past dawn.

I had to sit in that foggy field for nearly seven hours after having worked earlier that day for eight. The rims of my car sank into about six inches of mud, it was raining and it was cold. I was nowhere where I could get anything to drink, go to a bathroom and I was out of smokes and trying to stay upright and awake in a car without reclining seats.

To top it all off I had a migraine headache, and the air smelled like airplane fuel, burnt bodies and cow poop.

All of that made worse when the dispatcher radioed to tell me that my relief was going to be very late. But like I said, it wasn't all bad behavior and heartbreak, there was the radio show that Sheriff Smith allowed me to do each week for four hours on WCOL, called "Jail House Rock With Deputy Rick."

The sheriff knew I missed my roots and although I didn't give it much thought at the time I think he allowed me to unwind at my old stomping grounds because he new I was under constant stress. That at least massaged my sanity glands and allowed a few hours each week away from the ugly stuff.

And as ugly as the stuff I have written about was, there was something far uglier going on within the halls of justice every day.

Although politics inside of surrounding law enforcement agencies can get rather nasty. But uglier at times than all of that was the scandals within. Officers charged with theft in office, receiving blow jobs in their cruisers, other sexual activity among officers and inmates that were investigated as criminal cases, abuse of power, domestic violence and even a highly publicized badge selling scandal that saw a Chief Deputy convicted of a felony.

Then came the election of a new sheriff and my final two years with the black shirts. Two years in the Communications Center, way less glamour than the job I had under Earl Smith, but in ways that are hard to explain way more stressful.

Working in the radio room, or as I used to describe it, being held hostage at work.

Nowhere else in the sheriff's office is there a more demanding and less thankful position to be in. (Except perhaps the jail.) Dispatchers in an atmosphere as busy as the FCSO deserve twice what they are actually paid, and are the first to be blamed when things go wrong on the outside.

I really do not know how I kept my sanity for those two years.

I have often described my departure from the Sheriff's office as like winning the lottery when I received my commission with the Obetz Police Department. Out of the radio room and back into a patrol car and the duty to actually do work that was not only more rewarding emotionally, but came with better benefits and more pay.

Moreover, a chance to rise through the ranks, as I did.

Something that was never on the table in the S.O.

Although it was back to directing traffic in the frost of winters and the heat of summers, and back to pulling up on deadly crashes and binders full of other incident reports it was where I could grow old in the job gracefully.

In the Obetz P.D. I found a tight nit group of officers that for all intent and purposes got along very well, and I could not have worked anywhere for a better Chief of Police, or Mayor. Chief Francis "Bo" Smith was a jewel from the old school, a retired Deputy Chief from the Columbus Division of Police who was spending another dozen years as the top cop in Obetz, and the Honorable Mark Froehlich an ambitious mayor who was dedicated to bringing the town into the 21st century with as good a police department as he could assemble.

Unlike mayors before or after him, law enforcement was a top priority. He inspired cops to be better, to be more down to earth and to be more community oriented and less "gun slinger." Before Froehlich the towns P.D. was more known for its cowboy image and the town itself was thought of by outsiders as a speed trap.

I could not wait to get started when I received the phone call telling me that I was to receive my commission down there.

As an Obetz police officer, I quickly learned not only the town's history and its quirks, but who the good guy's and bad guys were, as well as who the monkey wrench throwers of village politics were. Sometimes the latter group was more aggravating than the lawbreakers were.

These were adults who saw themselves as way more important than they were, people who had a hard on for cops and sought daily ways to complicate not only their duty, but their personal lives as well.

People who would phone in phony complaints to the mayor's office, follow officers nightly with video cameras hoping to catch them misbehaving and even going as far as to write anonymous letters to officers wives accusing their spouses of infidelity.

What annoyed me more than the tactic itself was when they accused me of playing around they would name women that were not only not my type, but women who were no ones type. Usually it was women that the accuser himself was involved with, and sometimes they would get their girlfriends to go along with the lies.

Still, it did sometimes cause problems for some of us, both at work and at home. And that's all these people wanted from their efforts anyway. Most of them were rookie troublemakers by comparison to what I had on my plate in the county, but just enough to distract from time to time from what was the perfect job for a police officer.

And because they were small time operators, I won about 95% of the challenges they tried to pose. Sometimes I actually enjoyed finding ways to stay ahead of the curves that were tossed at us. Diversions from an otherwise sometimes too serious atmosphere.

None of that lessened my gratefulness to be away from the sheriff's office and to be back on the street. When I was a third shift patrol officer I looked forward to going to work every night. From the minute I walked out of roll call, to loading my cruiser for the night, to most of the miles I would drive, and even the paperwork I would do each night, I rarely thought of that job as work.

And only once can I remember thinking I would rather be somewhere else besides working, that was the final Christmas Eve I could have had with my mother before she passed away, and knowing it was going to be her last.

I spent that entire night thinking about it, driving that cruiser up down the streets of Obetz, tempted to head north to be with her. I found my solace knowing she understood, and that she would want me to carry out my responsibilities. Still, it was the one time I considered going AWOL from my duties.

But for most other nights, any tour of duty with no car crashes or violence of any sort was a good night, and that was most of them.

And by two in the morning if something bad had not happened it wasn't likely to, that meant a lot of down time to get to just patrol the neighborhoods and get to know snitches, study the landscape of what your paid to watch, remember which vehicles belonged where and which one's were in places the shouldn't be.

It afforded time to meet with and form bonds with other officer's from other jurisdictions in the area like officer's from the Groveport P.D. and from Madison Township, Columbus P.D. and State Highway Patrol. The chance to learn from the more experienced one's and to know that if anything ever got bad enough to scream for back-up it would be those friends who would rush to your aid.

There is no way I can describe the tranquility of pulling into a dark parking area of the at 3:00 AM to finish paperwork or to study new changes in or additions to the Ohio Revised Code or to just meet up with another officer to discuss earlier event's or to engage in small talk to help each other stay awake.

No way to express the joy of playing practical jokes on other officers like seeing them inside of a gas station loafing and flirting with a clerk and while their back was turned placing road-kill under their car seat, rolling up their windows and turning the heater on full.

Or setting their car radio on a hip-hop station and turning it up as loud as possible so their cruiser would thump like some ghetto machine. Customers going in and out of the store would walk by and laugh, perhaps wonder, "how hip is this cop?"

I would not trade those early years as a patrolman for any other era or job I ever had, but I would have gladly traded my final few years as Chief of Police for them. Anyone who has ever supervised cops probably understands that.

Mack the Knife

A round St. Patrick's Day in 1978, I was the all-night DJ at WMNI-920-AM. I am pretty sure that it was actually the night of St. Pat's Day when a fellow announcer was slaughtered one floor below where I was working. His name was Jim Eldredge; he hosted a talk show, which aired immediately before my over-night program.

The WMNI studios were in the Great Southern Hotel at Main and High Streets in downtown Columbus, and Jim not only worked there on the seventh floor, he lived in a suite on the sixth floor.

As was his habit, after finishing his program he crossed High Street to a favorite pub of his for an evening of whatever he routinely went there for, then around 3:00 AM he returned to the hotel - stopping by the studio where I was doing my program.

We exchanged our usual dialogue and he went off- to his violent death as it were.

Little could I have known that morning that I was probably the last friendly person Jim would see. At least as far as I know the last co-worker. After finishing my program, I got onto the elevator and not uncommonly, it stopped on the sixth floor on the way down.

A tall black man, wearing a dark trench coat, and a furry hat, got on and the elevator expressed directly to the first floor where I got off and left the building. As I left, it dawned on me that my fellow elevator passenger was a little odd.

However, the fact that I shared the car with him was not.

In those days, The Southern Hotel was not known for its higher-class clientele as it is today. It was not unusual to find freaks hanging around at any hour.

Prostitutes, alcoholics and the like were common pedestrians in and out of the hotel. And the fact that this particular individual had what looked like aviator glasses on did not signal anything strange.

Nor did his untied combat boots. He looked like anyone else who might make others nervous in an elevator car in a run-down hotel in the early morning hours. I was used to it.

That is until I returned to the station later that day and saw several police personnel milling around with their clipboards and cameras. I ran into another announcer who told me that Jim had been found murdered in his suite.

That announcer was Ron Barlow.

Ron was the stations franchise announcer, one of the most popular broadcasters in Columbus. I could tell by his expression and by the tone of his voice that he was not putting me on. Even though it would not have been too weird if he had been.

Jocks liked saying stuff like that about other jocks. It is a warped fraternity sometimes.

Nevertheless, as the circumstances unfolded it was true. Jim had been stabbed something like sixty times. Those who were allowed into his room after the police finished their work described the scene as looking like a slaughterhouse. Blood on the walls, the ceiling, the furniture etc.

The cops had no immediate suspects. They wanted to talk to as many co-workers as necessary, and I, as the one who had seen him last was someone "of interest."

However, not for long.

I did tell him or her about the stranger who joined me on the elevator but they did not seem too interested in him, and I was left with a feeling that they had suspected one of us, maybe another announcer.

Because of this, working the over-night shift took on a different emotion for me.

Back then, I was the only WMNI employee in the building after midnight. As a matter of fact, the only hotel employee in the building during the overnight period was the desk clerk downstairs. So coming to work each night knowing there was a killer running around somewhere was just a little spooky.

Especially during those times when I would have to leave the locked studio area and pass the elevators to go to the bathroom. Sometimes I would glance at the wall panel and see the elevator lights indicating that it was coming up. Sometimes it would stop on our seventh floor and no one would be on it.

It was times like this that I ducked back into the secure confines of the studio area and forget that I had to go. I think after awhile some of us began to look at each other suspiciously. Wondering if one of us might be the cold-blooded killer of Jim Eldridge.

And since several months were passing with no arrest it became increasingly worrisome that the killer might never be identified.

Thankfully, an arrest was made, nearly a year later.

The police arrested a tall black man and charged him with Jim's murder. It was explained that Jim had met the man at the bar, and it was believed that he brought him back to his apartment where it was clear some sort of fight erupted.

Whatever went wrong Jim was killed for it.

In the years that passed, the memories of that incident seem less important, as sad as that sounds. Nevertheless, it remains one of the most vivid memories I have.

From our boss, Mr. Mnich who was the unfortunate one to find that gruesome scene, to anyone who might have teased or chided Jim about his old fashioned style of announcing, to the sales people who found it easy to persuade clients to buy time on his program, to those who admired and respected his experience, and even the front desk secretary who cared about all of us.

Yet in the shadows of all of that seriousness, one DJ on staff could not resist joking about it. Knowing that Jim was cremated after he was killed he would remark anytime someone emptied an ashtray… "Hey don't dump that…"never mind, you get it. Radio people could be brutal.

Since then I have lost many friends from that station. Mr. Mnich himself passed away in 1981 the morning after our staff Christmas party. Later our news director, Martin Petree, our program director, Steve

Rick Minerd

Cantrell, morning man Bill Weber, Carl Wendelken, newsman Tom Allen and others.

I worked for WMNI for about six more years following Eldridge's murder. And even though I honestly feel that was the best job I ever had, I can never forget that night in 1978. Sometimes when I enter that building still today, I remember as if it were a recent event.

Knowing that as I was probably joking around that night, on the air, or with a listener on the phone, having and enjoying the time of my life playing country music while a friend was experiencing Hell just a few feet below me.

Red Necks, White Socks & Blue Ribbon Beer

When it was legal in Ohio to consume alcoholic beverages at age 18, albeit 3.2 beer, going out in Columbus for those of us old enough to close out the 1960's it was either the campus areas pub's or those all over the Eastside.

Few in my generation do not remember the Lavender Pussycat, the Driftwood or the Boathouse or Pandora's Box for a taste-o-the hop's and barley, or Kuenning's or Emil's for chow, if there was a date hanging on. Pat Zill's Boathouse was where I first saw a major star on a tavern's stage.

I would eventually see many more on campus at the usual spots, but The Boathouse was Pat's place and he was as well known in Central Ohio, if not better known than most local rockers.

Pat could sing anything, and most of the time when he sang songs that were also famous by other artist's he sounded better, regardless of the genre. I only saw him as a fan in my early radio career but I got the opportunity to meet him when I went to work for WMNI.

In those early years, the station hosted weekly live country shows, (The WMNI Country Cavalcade) in the Southern Theatre on Saturday night's. And early on, DJ Ron Barlow hosted most of them.

But as the years went by it was taken over by Carl Wendelken and soon after, all of us had opportunities to emcee not only many great local performers, but national acts as well. Pat was both. It was at the Cavalcade where I met him.

If he were on the Saturday night card, it was as if every listener WMNI had wanted tickets. Looking back on the past four decades and being reminded of these people and places, I feel compelled to catalogue as much as I can about them.

Summertime Blues

1967 was special for me. Not because it was the so-called "Summer of Love," as a matter of fact I don't remember anyone calling it that until years later. For me it was more about making money in as many way's as I could to save up for my first car, a 1960 Ford Falcon. I had no time for girls. Not ready yet.

Worse than that, they had no time for me. However, I managed to struggle through that summer counting down the days until I could get my driver's license and customize that Falcon. Then the girls would frown for having ignored me all of those years.

Most of the money I did make was from delivering the Columbus Citizen Journal Newspaper. About ten bucks a week. There were some lawn mowing and other odd jobs in there, but unlike my paper route, I did not enjoy those "careers" as much. I did however like delivering newspapers though.

Except for one particular morning. I had stopped on my way home after delivering my last paper and gotten my morning donut and chocolate milk from Berkey's Bakery on East Whittier Street, and I had gone across the street to sit on the fire escape of Heyl Avenue School to eat when I noticed an old green Rambler circling the block.

I did not give it much thought at that moment, I was fourteen years old and really never worried about things like that, I doubt that I even suspected what was on the guys mind. But a few minutes later, he pulled his car alongside my bike as I was heading home and he asked if I had any extra papers. I told him no, and then he asked if I could handle a blowjob.

This may sound strange, but the first thing that went through my mind was a similar incident that happened when I was about eight or nine years old. Then, while walking home from the Marham Theatre on High Street with my brother and sister and a few neighbor kids, a man began chasing us and actually caught me and was dragging me toward his car. I do not know how I got away from him then, but I knew I should get away from this guy now.

I rode away as fast as I could and eventually saw my paper manager and flagged him down and told him what had happened. He followed me the rest of the way home and within a few days the incident was forgotten. Still, green Ramblers made me nervous anytime I saw one.

With apologies to the Columbus Dispatch, I knew that I was delivering the best newspaper in the history of Columbus. Up at 4:30 every morning, riding through quiet streets, hearing the echoes of the paper as it slid across wooden porches and slammed against a door, throwing it as hard as I could on purpose at the doors of customers who rarely paid for it on time, my childhood.

However, back to "The Summer of Love." Bobby Kennedy was still on the horizon for hope, every American car maker had exciting rides in their show rooms, some of the best television shows ever were in their prime-and TV was free.

The radio was awesome. "The New WCOL" had no peers. In addition, my ten bucks a week allowed me to not only save money, but could keep me busy all week. More important than all of this, the most exciting years of my life were just getting started, and would end before I appreciated them.

Life itself being wasted on the young and I did not even know it. I did not care because I never expected that period to end.

The Joker

From time to time, I try to take a break from being so serious and reflect on incidents that for a lack of a better way to describe them were a bit juvenile in nature. Like when cops get bored because everyone is behaving on the roadways, no one is fighting, thieves are stealing in another precinct and perverts are relaxing at home with their blow-up-dolls because they struck out prowling the streets.

Rare occasions all of them. However, nights like that do happen once in awhile. On those nights when the radio was silent and the other Cops did not have any new war stories to share while parked side-by-side waiting for anything to keep us awake, some of us would discuss creative ways to mess with other Cops.

Like those guys from the Columbus Police Department who used to pick up drunks in their jurisdiction and drop them off in ours. Or the bogus calls a cop might make from a pay phone to the radio room asking for an officer to check out a naked lady walking down Williams Road.

That was fun, because it seemed every deputy sheriff, state trooper or city constable would mark "in route" when the dispatcher would say, "Any car in the area?" They came from miles away, in droves.

Of course there was no naked lady, sometimes it would be a drunk on the side of the road puking. Sometimes they would find a dead deer blocking traffic and get stuck removing it. Another fun activity was seeing another police car parked outside of an all night convenience store and the cop inside drinking coffee and flirting with the clerk.

We could get on the radio and ask for that officer to "check up." As if we were worried about him. Or, we could ask radio to have him meet us somewhere several miles from that location. Then when he left, we would go in and drink his coffee, probably flirt with his girlfriend.

Another trick was before he got into his car we would reach into it and turn on his air conditioner if it were winter or his heater if it was a hot night. We would also adjust his radio to its loudest setting, turn on his FM radio to loud static between stations, or put one of those signs in their windshield that says "Help, Call The Police."

Nevertheless, the best was to find road-kill and shove a carcass under his seat. After a few hours of driving around it would render the car and its driver stinky. However, going that extra mile always brought consequences later. Someone who would do such a thing would have to go over every inch of his own cruiser every time he got in it.

Every one got paid back some time, some how.

Sometimes weeks would pass with no repercussions, but then, when least expected, one might open his car door to find that another officer had emptied his mace canister inside of it, or worse.

Timothy

Having the opportunity to participate in a popular nationally televised crime program was special in a lot of ways.

To be a part of assembling a true life story through re-enactment with network producers and directors, as well as some talented actors both on the professional level and others who happen to be friends on the sheriff's department was just the beginning.

Some days just happen. Such was the day when an executive producer from "America's Most Wanted" telephoned my office in the fall of 1991 seeking to make arrangements to interview a prisoner incarcerated in the Franklin County Jail.

As was Sheriff Earl O. Smith's policy to accommodate the media whenever possible we went through the necessary procedures to make this happen for them.

During the course of arranging for their interview I was asked if our department had anyone on the run that they could assist in apprehending. It just so happened that in the weeks previous we let one get away.

Timothy Brewster was in our facility on charges of rape, kidnapping and probably more when he devised and ultimately carried out a plan to escape. He knew from having been a "guest" in our place that the county took inmates in need of medical attention to Doctors North Hospital.

So through letters and visits with his son he laid out a plan where he would cut his wrist and upon being taken to the hospital his son would be waiting to ambush the deputies escorting him and set him free. His plan worked. Brewster was on the run.

Within a few days of AMW's staff completing their original business with us their semi's full of production equipment arrived in Columbus to begin shooting the re-enactment of the case.

While they were unloading, I accompanied the producers on a scavenger hunt around the county for ideal shooting locations. While they set up to shoot scenes at the County Jail we were making arrangements to be let into the Old Ohio Penitentiary to document another of Brewster's former homes. Getting the co-operation from all of the other agencies to cut some film was almost as much work as filming it.

We needed the Ohio Department of Rehabilitation, The Columbus Police Department and their helicopter unit, patrol officers from their agency as well as some from the Franklin Township Police Department, Doctors North Hospital, someone's house that would resemble something Brewster would live in and a convenient store with a parking lot big enough to accommodate lots of movie making equipment and as many as one hundred people involved in a film sequence.

We also had to cough up some uniforms for the actual actors who would play roles in the project. One of the best actors on the set was our very own Lieutenant Alan Mann. Lt. Mann played the role of one of the deputies who actually apprehended Brewster in a robbery he committed when he was younger, and later he was a physician at the hospital. That ability to multi-task might be one of the reasons he is now a Major.

I have been around local television productions before and was impressed by how hard they work, but being involved with a network project is something to behold.

We shot several scenes many times over; we filmed in bright sunshine one day and in a driving rainstorm late at night the next.

It took nearly a week to finish a fifteen-minute segment. And when it was over and was scheduled to air on the Fox network I was flown to Washington D.C. to appear on the program with John Walsh. Like I said, some days just happen.

Within two weeks of the airing, Mr. Brewster was spotted in West Virginia by someone who had seen him on the show. He was apprehended and brought back to Franklin County where his charges now included escape.

I have not kept tabs on his whereabouts but I am guessing he is still locked up. His temporary reprieve lasted just a little longer than his sons did. He was caught the day after he helped his father get away.

Tommy

The apartment complex once called Greenbrier was the Wholly Grail of ghettos in the Columbus area. While working as a peace officer there I came to be pestered by a little blonde haired boy about eight years old each night asking my partner and myself for money.

His name was Tommy, and we used to find this kid out riding his bike that had no tires, just rims as late as midnight. In an area famous for violence. We always took him home and on occasion would find his mother passed out and clearly stoned, thus making it necessary to make other arrangements for Tommy's well being.

I felt sorry for this kid. At the time, my own children were small, and seeing the kids at Greenbrier made me understand how lucky mine were. They lived in a safe neighborhood and had luxuries that would never be enjoyed by the rag-a-muffins in Greenbrier.

I decided to make Tommy my personal project.

Through arrangements with Children's Services, my wife and I would pick him up and include him and his ten-year-old sister in some of our family activities. He and my youngest son Todd hit it off immediately because they were about the same age, as did his sister and my daughter.

Our family took these kids out to eat, to museums and all of the things we do as families. We even made Christmas possible by taking care of their holiday meals and gifts for both of them. Tommy got a bicycle with tires. In addition, my wife took him to her office Christmas party where she worked at the Franklin County Court House and he received even more presents and was befriended by a few Judges.

After several months, Tommy's family moved away and we lost track of his whereabouts and his well-being. However, several years later I found out where he ended up as an adult. In prison, on a murder charge.

It makes me wonder if he ever sat in his cell, pondered a moment in his childhood, and remembered that someone on the other side of justice at least tried to point him in the right direction.

Ashes to Ashes

D ust to dust. One of the coolest songs ever recorded was a semi-hit for The Fifth Dimension back in 1973. "Ashes to Ashes" was the tale of a neighborhood and a time falling victim to progress?

The lyrics told of reflecting on a place and era of innocence being lost, "They're tearing down the street where I grew up, like pouring brandy in a Dixie-cup, they're pouring concrete on a part of me, no trial for killing off a memory."

And, complimenting the story was a smooth blend of harmonizing and just the right music. I still quiver when I hear it.

It was the site of my first apartment, and like my friend Kcalb Nosnhoj Nomeeb whose name appeared on Dymo Tape on his front door just as I have shown it here, I too had my name on the front door in similar fashion. Drahcir Naed Drenim.

I admit to copying that. How cool! Egotistical enough to think if my name were spelled correctly my neighbors would somehow know, or care who I was. Sort of like hiding my identity by calling myself R. Dean on the air at WTVN-FM where I earned that two bucks an hour.

And in a complex where there were 1300 apartment units, mine too was on Bellwood Court. I swear that was a coincidence. It was not by design, it was by chance. In addition to moving into the same apartment complex, I drove a blue Buick Skylark not unlike his.

Chesterfield Apartments, as it was known back then is gone, demolished in 2007. Before it was torn down, it resembled a third world country. But what a treasure trove of memories I have from not only 3077 Bellwood Ct. Apt #2, but of the entire once quiet neighborhood.

In its heyday, the community was home for 5000 residents. The exact number a community must have to qualify to be a city.

I guess Judge Harlan Hale had no choice but to order it purged from the landscape.

Before it was named Chesterfield it was known as Beverly Manner. Built in the 1940s to house military families who had moms and dads employed adjacent to it at what was then called the Defense Construction Supply Company. (DCSC)

In its glory days it was quite beautiful. Picturesque, with its miles of winding, tree-lined sidewalks. However, by the 1980s the writing was on the walls. Literally.

Graffiti and gang signs that announced you have entered an extremely dangerous place. So bad in fact, that the owners of the complex hired the Franklin County Sheriff's Department to provide four deputies working in two patrol cars every night to keep some semblance of peace.

The complex where I had my first apartment became the training ground for my first patrol experience as a deputy sheriff. Its new name was Greenbrier. Or, as we called it, "Uzi Alley," named for the frequency of nightly gunfire.

In the year the sheriff's department was contracted there we locked up nearly 500 criminals on charges ranging from carrying concealed weapons, discharging firearms, buying and selling drugs, assault, theft, various traffic offenses and warrants for almost every violation in the Ohio revised Code.

While working there I could not help but reflect back more than a decade previously when that was my neighborhood. A place where I would take my young son Ricky outside in the early evening and watch him romp with our pup named DJ.

And of the pre-dawn hours when I would take DJ for a walk after finishing my late night radio shift at WBUK. Without worry.

I visited the area in the weeks before it was all gone, and although the entire community had been abandoned, the parking lots looked like they hadn't been paved in decades, the lawns had become overgrown with knee high weeds and the doors and windows had been removed from every building, I could visualize it's long ago beauty.

Even though the entire area was posted with "No Trespassing" signs, I had to step inside 3077 Bellwood Ct. #2 a final time.

As I walked around where more than thirty years ago I paid $135.00 every month to rent it, I thought about the blue shag carpeting that was once on the floor, the glass coffee tables and a checkered couch that came with it as a furnished unit, our black & white Philco television, the tiny bedroom that was DJ's lock-up while I was at work, the living room wall where I leaned a 14 -foot bass boat that doubled as a record shelf, and amazingly I found the same black and white bathroom tiles still on the floor.

What I did not think about that day was how that area earned the nickname "Uzi Alley." I chose not to.

The Worst That Could Happen

Imagine waking to find your four-year old daughter missing not only from her bed, but also from the house. It is not imaginable unless you have experienced such a horror.

We think we know what that would be like but I do not believe most of us can know what someone else feels just by imagining. And for the luckiest of us, we will never have such a theory tested.

I only experienced seeing a mothers such grief one time, and that is something I can never forget. The Franklin County Sheriff's Department was dispatched to such a case several years ago, and as the Public Information Officer at the scene I saw a woman kneeling in the street screaming for someone to answer the question, "Where is she?" "Where's my baby?"

It was just before dawn, and the screams were bone chilling.

Her toddler had been snatched from her bed sometime overnight while the family slept. What the investigation later learned was that a man had broken into the family vehicle and found keys to the house. As he went through the home, he found the little girl asleep and took her.

As the media descended onto the scene, we provided them with color photos of the girl and the pictures were rushed onto of the local television news programs. Luckily someone in Hocking County recognized the child from seeing her the previous day with an acquaintance who when asked why the girl was with him was told that he was baby-sitting. By this time, the girl had been found wandering around in a Columbus shopping mall where the kidnapper had brought her back to town and dropped her off.

Sheriff Earl O. Smith dispatched two detectives to Hocking County to assist deputies there in searching this guy's property, a farm out in the country. We had his name and address so our hopes of capturing him were high.

He also ordered me to go along to deal with whatever media attention might follow the story, especially if the circumstances went bad. So I accompanied Detectives Jerry Jodrey and Frank Kennedy with the hope that the tip was good and that we would find this guy and bring him back to Columbus to face charges of kidnapping, aggravated burglary and rape.

Upon arrival in Hocking County the three of us were deputized by the county sheriff and we were joined by four deputies from that jurisdiction and headed out to his farm. We had a photograph of him and a description of his vehicle, a blue 1965 Dodge pick-up truck.

We arrived at the farm and searched thoroughly, but to no avail. He was not there.

On the return trip back to the Hocking County Sheriff's office, we were discussing our disappointment when I noticed an old pick-up truck coming at us from the opposite direction. But it was not blue. The front of the truck was mostly primer gray.

Being pretty good at being able to name any vehicle made in America before the 1970s I noticed the headlights of the truck were rimmed by what looks like big, chrome pie-pans. Exactly the features of a 1965 Dodge.

And as the truck passed, I turned to look at it, and noticed the quarter panels and the tailgate were blue. I forget who was driving our car but it suddenly braked hard and did a donut to pursue what was our suspect. We radioed to the Hocking deputies who were leading us back to their headquarters that we were sure that was him.

They too made a u-turn and together we chased him back to his farm. Then, as he attempted to cross a muddy field, his vehicle got stuck. Chase over.

All of us surrounded the truck with our weapons drawn and ordered him from his vehicle. It was a moment our victim and her mother might have enjoyed. For when he refused to get out by stating he could not because his door would not open, our comrades from Hocking said, "No problem."

They reached through the window and pulled him out. By the hair.

When we got him back to the Hocking County Jail, I called our sheriff to tell him the good news. Sheriff Smith asked if the suspect had anything to say and I told him that he said he was glad he had been caught, and that he was ready to find Jesus. The sheriff said, "Tell him when he gets back to Columbus I'll help him find Jesus."

He did not mean kneeling with him to pray.

Devil with the Blue Dress On

B ack when radio was something fun to be on and something cool to listen to there were not many female DJ's on the air. They did not get a strong footing into the industry until I was well into my own career. In those days, it was mostly a *man thing.*

I remember the first time I heard a female spinning tunes and rattling off time and temperature checks on WCOL. Her name was Vicky Starr. I did not work with any female jocks until a couple of gals showed up to make their marks in country music radio. Pam Easterday, a conservative looking girl who was all business, and another one calling herself Cherokee. I thought they both made those names up. Only one of them did.

What I do remember is that they shook things up at the former all-male club at 920 on the AM dial. We were a bunch of redneck cowboys. It was almost as if we continued to say "Home of the Country Gentleman" on the air we'd risk bodily harm from these girls.

Where Pam was the more studious type showing up for work wearing business suit's straight out of Gentleman's Quarterly, Cherokee was the one who presented the biggest scare. I will have to admit that I resented her in the beginning.

Not because she was a female who was taking over a program that

I had poured all I had in to, but because when I went across the hall I hated my new job.

Mid-days on a station that could not decide if it wanted to be "Sunny-95" or "K-95". The format was a weird mix of everything from Sheena Easton to Willie Nelson. Not to mention I hated working in the daytime.

I was begging our program director to put the new guy on FM and send me back where I belonged. I never understood his reasons for denying that request until several months later. And by the time I understood it all, WCOL had answered my knock.

After leaving WMNI for a job at WCOL, I found myself working with another pair of female jocks. A scenario similar to the two at 'MNI. Where Suzy Waud reminded me of Cherokee, Pam Spencer was more like Pam Easterday.

The common denominator they shared was their wardrobes. I never saw any of them in a dress. I tried to imagine it, but it would have been easier to picture some of our dude jocks wearing one then it was to visualize them.

As a matter of fact, the only DJ I ever worked with who did show up for work in a dress once was the late Bill Weber. He even had an imaginary dog named Spot that he talked to regularly. It was odd to peer through the glass and see him asking the dog that was not there questions and barking back answer's to himself.

It was not uncommon to see Bill in drag, or for that matter dressed in other costumes and making as much commotion as possible to draw attention to himself.

He might don a wig, stuff his shirt with plastic balls, and go out and emcee live shows as Dolly Parton if he thought it might get a laugh. He liked to be noticed. He expected it.

Indian Reservation

R ick BrownEagle, was one of the most interesting men in Columbus radio. I don't believe he ever did any real broadcasting but he was always' around at WMNI Radio during my stint with that station. He was a fixture there. But he was no mascot.

When I first saw the man, he nearly scared me into a bathroom stall where I could have locked the door. Not that that would have saved me if he decided to draw down on me and open fire.

I was in the restroom one night shortly after I had been hired by the station, it was around 1:00 AM when this dark complected guy wearing a cowboy hat, boots and a holster tied around his thigh walked in. In his holster was a pearl handled .45, and around his neck was a leather necklace with a huge turquoise medallion.

He wore matching bracelets and a matching belt buckle. He had on a cowboy vest and was wearing jeans with the cuffs rolled up to the tops of his boots.

It was not Halloween so I did not consider that there might be a costume party somewhere in the Southern Hotel, and I could not think of any reason this Indian dressed like a cowboy would be in the WMNI bathroom at that hour of the morning. He never said.

I quickly left and went back to the studio locking the lobby door behind me.

A few minutes later I saw him come through the locked door. He had his own key. Not wanting to confront him, mostly because he was the only one there who was armed, I called our program director Steve Cantrell and told him about this visitor. Steve calmed my fears by explaining that the guy was our security chief.

Hell, why not?

I was new to Country music radio and was not familiar with all its customs and nuances. An Indian dressed like Matt Dillon, it made sense.

As I got to know the Chief, I learned that he had a fascinating background. The guy had been everywhere and seen everything. He knew everyone. As time went along, I looked forward to his late night visits.

"Chief" BrownEagle as he was known, fit right in with a cowboy radio station, I was not as sure that I did.

Girls Just Want To Have Fun

In 1993 when Franklin County Sheriff Jim Karnes assigned me to the Communication's Center to work as a dispatcher and 9-1-1 operator, nothing could have prepared me for the controlled insanity that I found there.

Although I was thrilled to be gainfully employed, and grateful to Sheriff Karnes for keeping me around in the post Smith era, it was the only speaking job I ever hated.

Chaos nearly every day, eight hours a day seeming more like sixteen.

We dispatched not only the sheriff's office, but also about a dozen other police agencies and a couple of fire departments as well.

Between multiple phone lines that never stopped ringing with sometimes-frantic callers screaming for help, and officers on any one of about seven channels needing information or instructions, peace was seldom in the room.

And sometimes, if there was a lull in the communications aspect of the environment, all Hell could break loose among the staffers at any given time, there was so much arguing and nit picking. Either between the com-techs, as we were called, or from the radio room Sergeant. In a room that sometimes had six officers working, they were usually broken up into cliques.

This group did not like that group and so on. As a result, there was limited opportunity to forge friendly relationships from within. It might have been the stress that came with the job, or the jealousies over who was sleeping with whom, or rumors and county folklore of such.

Moreover, if it *was* going on, it seemed the entire sheriff's office knew about it or heard some version of it. Then it would spread throughout the other agencies that were dispatched by the office. A buddy of mine who worked in there used to say, "If you sleep with one of these girls you had better be the best who ever did it, because everyone in Franklin County will know every detail of it an hour after you get up."

Even if officers were not sleeping with each other, there were rumors that they were. Sometimes those rumors seemed to start just to keep up the legend. It was like a reality show.

We had a female officer who would occasionally peel a banana very sensuously and swallow it without taking a bite. Watching her do it became something of a request by those who never saw it. I wanted to see it; it was somewhat cool in a twisted sort of way. But hey?

A few times after returning to my console after a break, I would find a woman's magazine opened to an article on how to please the man in your life. There was even a ruler that was passed around with names of different deputies and radio-techs strategically written on it.

If the guy was not that well known, or more likely, not that well liked, he might find his name around the one-inch marker. Occasionally one of the girls would leave two or three buttons of her uniform shirt unfastened, then pretend that it was necessary to lean over in front of the person trying to dispatch just to place something on the console.

They could be a flirty bunch.

One morning around 3:00 when the radios were silent, and the county was not screaming for help, a female com-tech called me over to her console and said, "Hey Rick, let me see your dick."

No one in the room responded, the comment was not off-the-wall, it was not unusual, or anything taken seriously and no one was offended, it was normal, radio room talk.

Her next comment was, "Never mind, let me see your pen."

"Damn people, someone say something in here, it's too quiet!"

Coming from across the room someone else was asking, "Does anyone have a banana?"

Some wives and girlfriends of some of the male techs were more than a little suspicious of them. It didn't help that a few would actually call their co-workers homes and ask for them, perhaps only to aggravate someone, or create suspicions.

A few times when I arrived at work someone would ask, "Did your wife tell you I called?" Once my wife got a call from one of the girls asking her to remind me to stop and buy some ice cream on my way to work.

But there were some in there who if they had not taken me under a wing and taught me the skills necessary to succeed in such a fast and complicated environment, I never would have survived that job at all.

I remember one of them who was my "coach" for about three months told me that the Sergeant had been concerned that I'd never learn everything that was needed to know in there, and she remarked back to him that I was "teachable."

Good thing I was not cursed with a bigger ego than I already had. Teachable? I was in my early 40's and had been a deputy for a number of year's by the time I was described as teachable.

However, I understood because it was taking a long time to get it all absorbed. There was so much to learn. But somehow this girl stuck with me and I actually became a pretty competent dispatcher. Not my idea of moving up the ladder of my chosen profession, but an experience that was probably good for me in the end. I lasted two year's longer than I had expected in that assignment.

Two years after beginning it, I left for a job as a patrolman in the Village of Obetz. Commercial radio was never this complicated.

Beauty's only Skin Deep

I have documented much of how I spent my time as a working adult in broadcasting and in law enforcement. But what I have not written much about is the ugly stuff that fills two thick scrapbooks' I have kept documenting two decades of the latter.

There was ugliness in both careers of course but ugly in different ways.

Broadcasting could be, and sometimes was ugly in a competitive way, in that jobs weren't often secure and pay was often low, and there were peers, sometimes colleagues working alongside each other lying in waiting to either trip the other one up, or just be in the right place at the right time if the competition tripped themselves.

Audience ratings, the sale of a station or the constant revolving management door that brought new programmers and other managing execs with new philosophies were often game changers as well. But cop work could get ugly in ways that unless you are a cop or have been one, there is no real way to explain how dirty the job often is.

A lot of cops would say that the nastiest segment of police work is the politics that officers have to struggle with just to do their jobs. Few cops would argue that.

Usually people who have zero or less clues about police work find themselves in positions where they can manipulate policy or stand in the way of getting things right. Usually that group enters the fold through elective process, for instance a mayor, a commissioner or a city council rep, but some can also gain authority by appointment, sometimes appointed not because they are qualified but because they are friends with the former.

But aside from the office meddlings that complicate an already "tense" environment there is the realty of "Out There." That place where the politicians who control the budgets and dictate policy know nothing about, nor could they find with Map Quest or with the most sophisticated navigation system in the world.

And even if they have watched every episode of "Cops" they still could not know or even have a clue about real cops do or what they navigate through on a regular basis. If they did, they would stay the Hell out of the way. I doubt that few would find the going as good as it looks on television.

I am sure they would find the smell less glamorous.

I can still recall the stench of the first homicide I ever stood over, in fact, everyone who ever stood over one can do that. Anyone who has whiffed the aroma of dead and rotting human remains can tell you it is one you cannot forget and one that as soon as you smell it again you know exactly what it is. This one was about 19 years old when she was found murdered and left like fertilizer, naked and rotting in a cornfield.

It was summertime and the detectives investigating estimated she had been there for more than a few weeks, perhaps a month. In addition to the toll taken on a body left lying in a muddy field for weeks during August, wildlife had been eating pieces of her rotting flesh and what they weren't getting blankets of maggots were finishing up.

The evidence found on what was left of the girl and around the immediate area made it clear that she died a horrible death, possibly gang related and clearly one of slow pain and torture.

Various instruments had been used to cause what had happened here. By the time she was being surrounded by deputy sheriffs in place of those she saw last, her blond body hair was still mostly in tact even though most of what had deteriorated into dried black flesh wasn't.

My thoughts when I first saw her went back to the classroom at the training academy when we were preparing to watch an autopsy on a person who had been dead for a while. It was there that I learned that all people, even us white ones turn black if after we die we are left "untreated."

Everything about that day would have been offensive to anyone who had to assume any role in either finding, cleaning up, figuring out or explaining to someone why there were so many sheriff's vehicles and guys with camera's and note-pads in a farmer's field. But even more offensive than the visual of what was found out there that day was the smell, the one that gets on everyone who does stuff like this for a living.

Driving home that night I wasn't giving as much thought to the girl or what happened to her, as I was about how I smelled horrible. The odor that had been absorbed into my clothing had also been absorbed inside the membrane of my nostrils, it just stayed with me.

I remember stopping at a red light and lifting my tie to my nose and realizing what I was taking home. When I got there, my wife ordered me out of the house. I smelled worse than raw sewage. Those around me said I smelled worse than that.

After stripping off my clothes in the garage and after several cycles through the washing machine the clothes had to be bagged and put into the trash. Nothing would make them smell polite again. A few days later, I stood with other deputies over another victim trying to formulate in my mind the words I would use to explain what another investigation was all about. The same thing, but not the same thing.

The Homecoming

Every summer in early August many current and former residents' of the south end come "home" when they make their way to the playground of St. Mary's School searching for familiar faces at the annual Homecoming Festival.

And for most, if not all of them it is a nostalgic experience that hopefully will at least mentally take them back to the bricked area's they played on as kids. To see old friends and remember good things with them, or to see former foes and remember, or swear they remember similar good things with them as well.

In spite of the Yuppie Paradise it is has become over the decades, the old 'hood still looks the same. What seemingly is not familiar is many of the people who should be. Some of the *kids* we grew up with now look as if time has paid them back for something awful they may have done in their childhood.

Like me, I must have done some pretty terrible things back then. Another sad reminder that our best is far behind us is asking each other "Are your parents still alive?" It seems we all ask each other that because we all knew each Other's Moms and Dads.

Too often the answer is no, yet many of us can remember as if it were only yesterday seeing them with us on these same grounds for the same reasons we are there now, and even if it's been decades since, those memories don't seem so distant.

I did not attend school at St. Mary's but most of my friends during the so-called wonder years of life did. Therefore, I, like many like others who attended public schools in the area consider myself an Alumnus of the Parish.

Where we went to school back then mattered no more than it does now, it is where we grew up and who we knew that still does.

Every August I look forward to the event. To see how many familiar faces from my own past have managed to outrun time, and to remind myself to never again wear shorts in public and to never consider owning an Hawaiian shirt, let alone wear one not tucked in.

Flags advertising the ravages of old age.

I wish my peers would stop reminding me of who we have become.

Last Night I Didn't Get To Sleep

Like when John F. Kennedy was assassinated and when the Challenger exploded shortly after take-off, I know exactly where I was and what I was doing on July 25, 1968. Big moment's in life that burn such indelible details into the brain don't happen often, but those that change us in some way do occasionally and we remember them forever.

I remember most of the details surrounding the first time I got laid for example.

My first job, my first bike and the first day I rode it without training wheels. This is about the first day it was legal for me to drive, provided of course I had a licensed driver sitting next to me.

July 26, 1968 would be my liberation day from bicycles and any other means of foot power for transportation.

My Dad, understanding my obsession for cars, especially ones made by the Ford Motor Company "sponsored" me to obtain a 1960 Falcon several months before my sixteenth birthday. He loaned me the money for the $150.00 price tag, with my sworn promise not to take it out of the yard until I got my temporary driving permit.

On July 25th, 1968 I was edgy. Driving, or make that being allowed to do it legally had become the single most important issue on my mind and I was one day away from being tested for the opportunity. I had studied the drivers handbook until I knew it from memory yet I still paced from bumper to bumper staring at the Falcon all day trying to imagine not passing the written test that would give me the authorization to get it out of the yard and out on the road.

I might have been more nervous about taking that test than I would be three years later sitting in a maternity waiting room waiting to meet my first son.

We were all car guys and the first to the BMV would have been the luckier of us and I wanted it to be me. So on the night of July 25th, I could not sleep. I may have nodded off a few times in fear that if I stayed awake I would be too tired to be tested but I know it was a long night. I finally decided to forego any effort to sleep and got out of bed a little before daylight.

I went into the yard and slipped behind the wheel of my car for one last imaginary ride thinking that in a few hours I would not have to fantasize about it any longer.

It is strange, I couldn't tell you what I did on the day before Kennedy was shot but I can tell you where I was and some of what I did on the day before I first drove a car legally. I do have the same yard though.

That wonderful old Falcon no longer sits in the back yard, but I have an exact 1/32 scale replicate of it on a shelf. The toy cost $150.00.

$150.00 doesn't go as far as it did in '68, but then again, what does?

How About That

When television and I were young, Jimmy Crum was like the sixth starter on the Ohio State Basketball team as well as its play-by-play announcer. He was like "Mr. OSU." To this day I cannot watch a Buckeye basketball game without remembering his iconic "How about "that!" which when shouted by Jimmy was more of an exclamation than a question. The 1959 to 1979 voice of the basketball Buckeyes was stilled on January 5.

It is hard to believe it has been more than thirty years since Jimmy Crum called his last "Barn Burner." The Dean of central Ohio sportscasters as he was known was eighty years old when he died, and he lived a broadcaster's fantasy life. Getting in on the ground floor of early television with one of the big three in Columbus and staying at the same company for more than forty years.

Being in a position to either know or just rub elbows with every major player in the industry during his tenure at WCMH, (WLW-C-TV) as it was known when many of us were growing up here. Not just the broadcast players, but also the players of all the sports that passed through here. And not just of the OSU variety but every major sports figure who had a reason to perform in Columbus over that four-decade span at channel 4.

As much as Crum was heralded as a broadcaster, he was hailed as the champion he was for his other passions, raising millions of dollars for the children's charities that made him choke up on camera anytime he talked about them.

From his Easter Seals telethons where I came to meet him a few times to his "Recreation Unlimited" projects and "Special Olympics" "Mr. Crum" was never really out of public view even after his retirement from television in 1993.

His loud and flashy sports-coats that were his very public trademark for years continued on stages and pedestals throughout our community on behalf of kids with special needs until the final weeks of 2008.

Little Green Apples

Every Parent hopes for the best of circumstances for their kids. We want them to grow up and find their way through exciting, enjoyable lives. And, of course we never stop worrying about them or doing what we can to encourage them to make us proud.

When we say the apple does not fall too far from the tree, we hope there is some truth to that. I have been lucky; the fruits from my tree are close. Although they would not want to be thought of as fruits. But I know I can get away with this analogy, they are a forgiving bunch.

My oldest son Rick has been a Franklin County Deputy Sheriff for nearly twenty years and he is a good one. A supervisor as a matter of fact. In his years as a detective, he even came to my aid when I was a police chief in another jurisdiction.

The Obetz police department had been working a homicide for a number of months with little chance for solving it, that is until my son and his partner, Zachary Scott, a deputy who went through the training academy with me, took on the case and figured it out within a few weeks.

The two kids I inherited by marriage when they were toddlers grew up to find their way into exciting adventures as well. Joe followed a path into law enforcement and currently patrols one of the busiest areas in

Franklin County. He is a Franklin Township police officer. His sister, Kelly is a banker.

Before handling other people's money, she managed a business where she worked for twelve years rising through the ranks from a high school kid to a businesswoman.

My middle son Kevin has kept the Minerd name moving around in the broadcasting industry.

When he was fifteen years old, he was Columbus' youngest DJ at WWCD-FM-101.

From there he followed into a place I called home for nearly eight years, WMNI, and now he has an exciting position with the Grand Daddy of them all, Clear Channel Broadcasting who happens to be the parent company of WCOL, WTVN and WNCI, three stations I called home during my own twenty year career in the business.

And then there is the youngest. Todd. He continues to keep me laughing while keeping everyone else around him confused with his unique personality. He graduated from high school where he majored in law enforcement and is hoping to move up to the next level and probably will when the time is right, but for now he seems content to enjoy what's left of his youth before he falls into the trappings of marriage and parenthood that his siblings have discovered.

So, I am lucky. All of my kids have made me proud. Sometime within the next few decades I will have left the planet but I will have left something behind that will be good.

By The Time I Got To Woodstock

If everyone who has claimed to have been at the Woodstock Music and Arts festival back in August, 1969 were really there, there wouldn't have been enough room in Bethel, New York to accommodate such a crowd. Half of the disk jockeys I had worked with through the years claimed they were there.

I did not make it. Something I would regret for years. By the time I got to Woodstock we were half a million strong, but I was twenty-five years late in getting there. I went for my own twisted reasons.

Like many other things I have done in my life it was a spontaneous thing to do.

A few days before the 25th anniversary celebration I started seeing television news coverage of people pouring into Saugerties, New York for Woodstock ll and I decided to head that way. I checked with every crybaby I had ever heard whine about missing the first one and I could not find one person willing to go with me.

So I packed my 1987 Ford Aerostar and headed up 71 North toward Buffalo.

I made great time too. Too trusting of a friends absolution that Saugertise was just "a little North of" the Bill's' training camp. And when I pulled into the first tollbooth in New York I asked the attendant how far I was from Saugerties. He said about eight hours.

As it turned out my friend was wrong.

It was about this time I started thinking, is it really worth continuing a drive across the entire State of New York just to satisfy a quarter century itch?

Spontaneously I headed east. The further I got the further I Got. I read that once on a psychedelic VW bus.

After driving the longest distance I had ever traveled outside of an airplane I finally found the stopped traffic I was looking for. Flashing freeway signs were warning motorists that the New York Thruway was "Closed To all Festival Traffic."

Tired and pissed off?

At each freeway exit sat a N.Y. State Patrol car blocking any chance of getting off in the tiny town of Saugerties.

Then it dawned on me, these guys are cops. So I pulled alongside a State Trooper and explained that I was a peace officer from Ohio and that I had already had a miserable day and asked if he could please allow me to exit. I presented my credentials and he waved me onto the ramp.

When I exited I ran into the same scenario trying to merge into traffic at the bottom of the ramp. The Trooper there advised me to pull into a McDonald's lot where the cops working the festival were parking their cars.

He then told me that I would have about a two-mile walk to the gates of Hell. That's what he called it. The man was a prophet. But what did I care, I had just driven thirteen hours and I was not about to turn around and go home.

By the time I reached "Tent City" there must have been a hundred thousand already pitched. It was around midnight and Mother Nature began unleashing a violent thunderstorm. I could hear Steven Tyler screaming off in the distance so I headed toward the main stage area where I finally started to feel like I made it to Woodstock.

The rest of that night and all of the next day sucked. I had lost everything I took with me. My blankets, my makeshift shelter, some money and I have blocked out the rest. I could not lie down; I did not have any provisions. So I decided what the hell? I will drag my soaking wet, muddy, skinny ass back to Columbus. I really was cussing myself like that.

Somehow, after hours of walking around in muddy fields I found the area where I came in and left my dream voyage. It was the dumbest idea I ever acted on. Disaster, from start to finish.

Nothing Compares To You

The WLW family of television stations many of us grew up with in Columbus, Dayton, Cincinnati and Indiana shared some of the programming that gave us people like Sally Flowers, Ruth Lyon's, Paul "Baby" Dixon and of course Gene Fullen.

I remember that they were under the Avco Broadcasting umbrella and I have a particular fond memory of an advertiser that played an important role in not only bringing these people home to us, but in my childhood, "Moores Stores."

I'll get back to that, but as I think back on the early pioneers of TV entertainers I can't help but wonder what Ruth or Sally might have thought if they could have had someone explain to them, television in the future, and if somehow TV hosts such as Rosie O'Donnel and Ellen DeGeneres could have been teleported back to their era for them to see.

Sally might look at Rosie's snarls and hear her viper like personality and think to herself, that by comparison, she had the looks of Marilyn Monroe and the personality Jackie Kennedy. Seeing how Ellen "dresses up" for her show wearing sloppy untucked shirts, mens trousers and boys tennis shoes, and hearing her stutter and weave the words, "uh, uh, and uh between her baseless dialogue, she might understand why she has to bribe her audience with gifts to keep them in their seats for an hour.

And, if either of these older women could have been told how much money Oprah would be making to host her daily tripe, maybe neither would have died. They might have found a way to live forever figuring, "Hey, if she is worth that much......"

Television today, by comparison to what it was, when it was a relatively new form of entertainment is horrible. No spontaneity and personalities who would not have even made a good guest on the earlier programming. If Gene Fullen could take something like bowling and turn it into successful a game show that had everybody watching, what does that tell you?

Thank God, Rosie is not in my face much anymore when I do have the set turned on, I cannot look at her. And thankfully, I am not a TV junkie. If I were, I might have turned to drugs and alcohol before the early 1990's.

This brings me back to those great Moores Stores.

In my neighborhood Moores was like the last great General Store.

Just down the street from another popular local advertiser on television in those days, "Cousins and Fern." Not unlike the small Department Stores depicted in many of the old black and white movies, Moores was about as family friendly as any retailer could be.

They had everything my parent's wanted and everything I needed. Think Wal-Mart if downsized to about the size of a Wal Greens, but with a better selection of merchandise. For me it was a great toy store and where I bought many AMT and Revelle model car kits. And, where one winter day my Dad took me to the Moores on Parsons Avenue and Rhinehard Avenue to buy my first new Bicycle.

It was a Saturday night and it had been snowing, and my parents were going to Moores for something they needed and I went along.

While they shopped, I was hanging around the bicycle display admiring this Maroon Murray, with chrome fenders, headlights built into the tank and a row of reflector's across the rear carrier. It was the Lincoln Continental of two wheelers.

That bike had a price tag of $54.00; about half of what my Dad earned in a week working for the old Swift's Premium Meat Packing Company, yet another popular TV sponsor in the early 1960's.

When my parents finished their shopping, a clerk walked over to me and asked if I would push the bike outside for a customer. When I got it out there, my Dad asked me if I wanted to ride it home in the snow or if he should put it in his trunk.

No kid would have chosen the latter.

It took forever to pedal through the snow and I can never forget the amazement I felt seeing my headlights reflecting off the snow. Every time I saw a Moores commercial after that I stayed glued to the television. Today's programming is a disaster.

If sponsors like Moores, Swift's, or Cousin and Fern, were still on, I would go to the kitchen for snacks during the entertainment segments and rush back to the living room for the commercials. It is a shame we did not all have video recorders back then to preserve the quality programming that may never exist again. But then, there is Dr. Phil and Jerry Springer, and all of those reality shows.

Inagadadavida

The "Iron Butterfly" was the roughest bar in Columbus, or so some would argue. I was never in it and can't recall where it was, but I do remember a hippie friend of mine once asking, "Anyone wanna go to the Iron Butterfly and get our asses kicked?"

Going to, or saying you went to that place was like announcing that you were fearless, ten feet tall and bullet proof. Down here on the Southside, we did have a few places with scary reputations, such as The Midnight Inn and the Triple L Lounge, both on Parsons Avenue.

Then there was the Sand Pebble on Lockbourne Road and a place called Don's Inn on East Whittier Street. The toughest place I ever wandered into during my youth was one on E. Main Street called "Joe's Hole." The place had an entrance that looked like a big hole. The entire entryway was round, and white skinny guys like myself had no business even thinking about going in for any reason.

However, in the mid 1970's I went there with a friend of mine who worked for a company called "Multi-Flo." They serviced the beverage taps in many of the bars.

My buddy was on 24 hour call for service run's when there was a problem with the tap's there one night and he asked me to go along, as if I'd be any kind of back-up if things went bad for him.

I remember on the way out there I was telling him about this other white guy I knew from South High School who went in there one night with some friends and left in an emergency squad shot in the stomach.

It did not faze him.

He reminded me that he had a few narrow escapes at the Iron Butterfly in the past and that by comparison "The Hole" was nothing. "Worry" he said, "If I can't get their taps fixed." Aside from some rats and cockroaches in the basement where the kegs were kept there was not too much to "The Hole's" legend. We were in and out of there in quick time.

Back to the 'Fly. As far as I can remember, it was popular with some of the local biker's and a few of the more interesting car club's in the area. I did know some of the local hood's who swapped stories about their adventures in there, but either I didn't have the pearl's to check it out for myself, or it just didn't sound like a fun place to go.

If I could locate my "friend" Pee Wee, I am sure he could impart some memories of the Iron Butterfly. Pee Wee *thought* he was the toughest guy I knew, he was almost like a family member. Always at our house and treated like my second brother by my parent's.

And from the time I was about 6 year's old until I was 17, I sort of looked up to him. He used to talk about the Iron Butterfly and how he was a feared regular there.

After he stole my 1959 Ford just before my eighteenth birthday and drove off into the sunset, I never saw him until one day in 2001. He was sitting at the counter at Tee Jaye's on Parsons Avenue. Looking worn out and a little beaten down, not at all like the swaggering tough guy I knew in my youth.

For a moment, I thought about reaching for my handcuffs or at least asking where my '59 Ford was, but I decided to walk away.

Sugar Shack

Those old enough to remember "The Shack" on North Fourth Street and 11th Avenue just east of the OSU campus probably have many stories they can tell about that popular watering hole. Almost everyone I knew spent many weekend evenings there in the late 1960's and early 1970's.

It was the first campus bar I headed to on the night of my eighteenth birthday. In those days, 18 was the legal age for consuming 3.2 beer, which by law meant that it contained less alcohol by volume, but in reality was just as intoxicating as its 6% alternative. There was no difference except for the color of the bottle cap.

And for what it was worth, most of us hung out with older guy's anyway so when the beer came to the table in pitchers ordered by those over 21 we all drank the 6% stuff most of the time anyway. This bar was an exciting place in an exciting time.

The world was crawling with Hippies and a large segment of that culture in Columbus practically lived at "The Shack." Or so it seemed.

The music era was the best it has ever been in history, morals were more relaxed than anytime before or since, and few could be shocked by much of anything. It was commonly believed that if you could not get laid at the Sugar Shack you just could not get laid. And that is what a lot of us were there for in the first place. Some got laid on the electric dance floor. Or later when the indoor pool was installed.

In those days, no one needed to shout, "Show me your tits." To see *"Girls Gone Wild" we did not need spring break.*

1970 was a great time to have whisker's and long hair, and a great time to appreciate hard rock music, be willing to wear the flag as a bandana. Getting married, having kids and competing in the working world was my pay back for 1970.

In '70 I was on something of a sabbatical from the real world.

Instead of finding things to do to make life better I was finding my way to places like The Electric Playground on Lynn Alley where you could pay the one dollar cover charge to go in and drink and listen to Alice Cooper. From there it was the High Street Strip with the Hiedelberg North and South, the Castle and all points between.

And when my car would start and stay running, I could go as far out as The Bistro on Olentangy and spend another dollar to see the regulars there, Kenny Rogers and the First Edition. Then on a really good night, J.D Blackfoot would be calling them in somewhere.

Looking back, what really sucked was 1970 only lasted a year. For as much as it taught me, it should have lasted at least until 1980.

Old Days

When I watch Channel 10 now I am always nostalgic for the old guard, guys like Dave Layman, Lou Forest, Joe Holbrook, Tom Ryan, Lee Vlisides and the many others who shared focus on the cameras and brought the daily information to us.

With respect to all of the new faces on television now, none can replace the folks we watched while growing up or in my case, people we simply paid attention to and respected.

As a radio personality, I used to listen to all of the other announcers, comparing myself with them or listening for something I could "borrow" from their styles. I think a lot of us did that.

Layman was one of those smooth reporters whose style I sometimes tried to imitate while working at radio stations that expected us, the Disc Jockeys to also read news headlines and do in depth weather reports during our music shows.

I thought Dave and Lou were among the best anchormen ever in Columbus.

Jerry Revish and Cabot Rea seem to be the torches now, (not to diminish the number of other talents still around.)

I have learned that following his tenure here Dave went to work for KXAS TV in Dallas Texas, which was a major step up in that they were in the top ten television markets in the country. Some years later, he was in Baton Rouge at another television Goliath, WBRZ TV. Today he lives in Rhode Island with his wife and two daughters.

Dave's TV travels have included WLNE TV and WJAR TV in Providence, and he now spends his TV time as a panelist on a PBS program called, "The Lively Experiment" a program that looks at the news and how it's delivered and speaks to it's content.

Dave Layman is one of those people who was probably expected to move on from our viewing landscape because he was one of those guys who just seemed to have everything going for him. Having read his bio, I am not surprised that after all of these years he is still connected in a manner that seems to make sense. Having been through the doors of reporting, to managing the news, he has earned a place where we would all like to end up, being remembered for good work.

Ain't No Mountain High Enough

Before digital dial positions on FM radio, it was common for station's to promote themselves by rounding off to the nearest whole number. For example, 92.3 WCOL FM was hawked as Stereo Rock 92. Some stations still do, like the chick rock station, "Sunny95" and the Classic Rock station Q-FM-96.

WNCI was Stereo 98. They were the third "hip" station in Columbus. First was WCOL AM 1230 when they launched their rock format in the 1950's, then in the late 1960's WCOL-FM, the first progressive rock station came out from under it's boring religious format to feature rock album cut's and slick hippie DJs.

'NCI was still in its infancy and still just an FM station. In those days, AM radio was king. But by the early 1970's, under the genius of Program Director E. Karl and Station Manager Phil Sheridan, The Great 98 became what they advertised, "The Mountain of Rock."

Somewhere between the lightening pace of 1230 AM and the cool delivery of 92 FM with it's music format, and depending on the time of day there were similarities between all three stations on-air personalities.

Whatever it was, it started clicking before the mid '70's.

And as the popularity of FM grew WNCI and the new kid on the block, WLVQ-FM-96 forced WCOL FM to step aside and make room for the FM version of WCOL AM, WXGT, or 92X. However, before that came to pass, when 'NCI was making the AM rocker take notice there was a fiercely fought competition for the young Top-40 market. I was stuck at WTVN watching from the sidelines as WNCI and WCOL AM duked it out.

I had dreams of making it to WCOL until I got a call from my old DJ chum Beemon J. Black one night.

Beemon had previously worked at WCOL but had disappeared for a few years into another radio market and I had lost touch until that night. When he called, he said something about WNCI having this great new DJ working 7:00 PM until Midnight and he wanted me to thread a tape and record him and send him the tape.

So that evening I plugged my reel-to-reel recorder at home into my stereo and turned on WNCI. Beemon was this great new DJ. He had returned to Columbus. And because he was my former best friend in the business I was thrilled.

A few hours into his show I called him at the station and asked where he'd like the tape mailed to and was told to bring it to him at "Scots Inn" the motel at Morse Road and Sinclair Road where the 'NCI studios were located.

"The Mountain Of Rock." Now I wanted a piece of it.

I switched my efforts of trying to get on at WCOL to joining my old friend at "The Great 98." With his help, I got there at the right time for my age, the stage my career was in and for what WNCI was on the eve of accomplishing. That was to become the most exciting radio station in Columbus. I was 22 years old and up on top of a mountain.

Our core audience was high schoolers to college kids so it was easy to relate to and connect with our audience. Playing the best Rock music of the era and helping to blaze the growing popularity of FM radio on a hip station with hip management was more fun than was probably allowed by law.

And like Beemon muttered to me when I asked how he and I ended up together at the coolest spot on the dial "ain't no mountain high enough to have kept us off."

Translated, I think we both wanted that more than we ever wanted any other job. That is what I say to kids today when I speak to them about their dreams. What you want is out there for the taking. After WNCI, I found ways to *take* other segments of my life.

To do that it helps to being willing to do more than your expected to, say what needs to be said and find that alter ego that lives within even if it's a stranger to those who think they know you.

For me it has been my split personality that has rescued most of my dreams from failure. The goals you hope to reach are reachable even if that mountain looks higher than it actually is. My resume is complete. My life on the other hand still holds a few mysteries.

The Piano Man

Those of us who grew up on such innovative television programming such as Casper the Camel might remember the piano player for that show, Bill Palmer.

Bill also had his own early morning talk show on channel 6 at 8:00 that featured interviews with the popular celebrities of the day including the God of all talk-show hosts, Johnny Carson, fitness guru Jack LaLanne and Virginia Graham among them.

I also remember the Virginia Graham talk program that like Spook Beckmans' "Coffee Club" was something like "Must watch TV" for my own stay at home mom.

I have vivid memories of one particular show she did when Columbus Mayor Maynard Sensenbrenner washer only guest. The Mayor might best be remembered by his signature slogan, "Columbus is the most dynamic city in America." Sensenbrenner was the first politician I remember who always' had an American flag on his lapel.

A fiery politician who was highly sought to appear on several national programs.

I met Bill's daughter through on the internet and continue I learned that he, like so many other's in early live television got his start in radio. He began his radio career in Johnstown, Pennsylvania, yet another reminder for me that we do indeed live in a small world.

My own heritage, that is, the Minerd family migrated this way from that area.

A web site authored and managed by a "distant cousin", Mark Miner, called Minerd.com details some amazing historical facts about that side of my extended family.

Bill Palmer would have known one of my favorite early TV personalities, Chuck Nuzum well. In fact, I am sure he knew all the local TV people, those guys were a close fraternity. Bill's daughter Pam told me that following his television day's he returned to radio at WHOK, another station that has sent many well-known announcers in and out of television here in Columbus.

Not surprising to me that these guys who made name's for themselves on the video box made their moves back into radio later in their careers. I remember Spook Beckman saying often after his long run on local TV that it was good to return to what he called, "the theatre of the mind," radio.

It was there he said that one could really be themselves.

Be more creative and leave more to the audience's imagination.

Pam talked about her own childhood with a famous Dad, how when out in public people would approach him for an autograph and what it was like to meet other great "stars" such as Gene Fullen. I had totally forgotten Gene's days of playing Santa Claus for the kids at Christmas, (she reminded me of that) but not of his days of hosting "Bowling for Dollars."

Alice's Restaurant

One of the best, and to date most famous tales to come out of 22 South Young Street, the former home of WCOL has been often told about Neal Martin. One of my best friends from "childhood" or as I fondly remember it, my radio career.

In the early 1970's the greatest cuss word ever stated out loud was said to have been spoken by Neal on WCOL-FM as the song, "Alice's Restaurant" ended.

The legend (and this is truly a legend) is that Neal was on the air one night, and was either talking to someone on the phone, or was otherwise distracted, when the long version (twenty-plus minutes) of Arlo Guthrie's iconic tune was over, Neal said on open mike, *"What a great fucking song!"*

The Holy Grail of broadcast disobedience, a beautiful thing when gotten away with. Neal did it, and I have tipped my hat to him for years. I still smile every time that story is told, I laughed when I went back to proof read this story. Neal's legacy only gets stronger and more appreciated with passing time.

This story is talked about every time two or more people who knew him get together and discuss the great moments of Columbus radio; it is about what we all wanted to be, talked about. Neal was like a poster boy for progressive rock radio, and his famous *slip* ranks nearly as high as some of the lore that has surrounded Columbus' first rock jock, Doctor Bop.

WCOL-FM was the groundbreaker for Album Oriented Rock.

In its early days it carried what was referred to as God Squad programming all day but would eventually share hours with the rock guys, eventually giving way to a full-time alternative To AM radio pop.

Those who grew up listening to it, or who were adult enough to appreciate the difference between Top-40 radio and the progressive version of it know that there has never been anything like it since its morph into other formats.

From being the coolest station in town with it's revolutionary rock format to the teeny-bop WXGT-92X it would become, then back to WCOL as an oldies station to now sadly, a Country Music station, it like Neal was a true pioneer. WCOL-FM with its country format makes sense for a company in the business solely to make money.

But if anyone would have told us thirty five years ago that a station as famous for the Hippies that built it, as it was for the hard rock music they played would someday replace head banging guitars and synthesizers with twangy steel guitars and fiddles, few would have thought it would be possible

WKRP (In Cincinnati)

A letter I received from an old WRFD colleague one day a few years
ago brought back many memories of a pretty good radio staff,
and how some of us compare the people a lot of us worked with to the
fictional radio staff of WKRP. In fact, WRFD had a receptionist back
then named Loni Anderson!

Whether any of us were really like the actors on that show, it could
be agreed that we all knew someone who reminded us of every single one
of them.

Mark Baer, a newsman and later Sports Director at WRFD was
actually a member of one of the best radio staffs in Columbus at the
time. I won't say who reminded Mark of Les Nessman.

Former WSYX Channel six Newsman Jon Griener was the News
Director and along with fellow newsmen, Mike Beard and Ron Powers,
the stations personality staff consisted of Spook Beckman, Bill Stewart,
Denny Nugent, Damon Sheridan, Dave Winters and myself.

Winters was the Program Director who hired me, and the guy who
"trained" me there.

My first day on the air with him was an early Saturday morning and
I will never forget what Dave pointed out as the "most important" switch
in the main on-air studio, it was one that monitored WCOL-FM. He

explained that if he listened only to WRFD's music all day he would go crazy.

"This will keep you upbeat" he said, explaining that if I got bored playing Benny Goodman and Hugo Montenegro songs I could turn up the "Col monitor and stay upbeat with Ten Years After and Grand Funk Railroad music. After explaining a few more things about the studio, Dave was gone, leaving me to figure the rest of it out.

Dave Winters might have been a little like Andy Travis and I am sure most of the sales staff had a little Herb Tarlik in them.

And something that remains a fond memory for me was the stations physical characteristics, located in a picturesque setting on Powell Road and Route 23 in a building that reminded me of an old colonial style mansion. Meticulous and well manicured landscaping, with a sprawling lake on the grounds.

Back before Southern Delaware County and especially that particular intersection became the congested area it is now. Going to work there was like taking a drive to the country.

As I reminisce and write about the old days of Columbus radio and the stops I have made along the way I continue to be reminded of some pretty good people and of a time that will never again be as simple.

I'm Into Something Good

The subject of payola still comes up in conversations about radio, and how some of us either took money or favors for playing certain songs. A little "something extra" for on-air "favors."

It was not as prevalent in my time as it was in the 1950's and '60s, but it did exist, as it might still today. For anyone not familiar with what payola is, it is accepting money, usually from music promoters to make sure certain products get more than its normal share of on-air exposure. Or, in other cases, "plugola" money for clever ways to plug something a few more times than has been paid for.

I remember that some thought Spook Beckman must have been getting something for those three and a half minute endorsements he used to make for companies who had only paid for 60 seconds of commercial time, but I never believed it. That was just Spooks way of doing live commercials. I *think*.

Although a lot of free food used to show up in the WCOL "window" where the Spook broadcasted each day. As did beautiful satin jackets, ball caps coffee mugs, stuffed animals and t-shirts, all with company logos. So much stuff that Spook would pass it out to the staff.

I once asked him if he had ever accepted any form of payola in his long career and he asked me to explain what that word meant. He said he had never heard the word and was sure I made it up. "But", he said, "That's an interesting concept."

As for me, the closest I ever came to accepting anything was free food from Tee Jaye's Restaurant every Friday night. It was part of a package that a WMNI sales rep had worked out with them. Tee Jaye's paid for commercial time on my show, and the commercial they got was me calling them to ask what was on the menu.

Usually I would interview the owner, Nita Sokol. Nita was a sweet woman who would go along with my silliness when I would pick something from the menu and ask if she could bring it to me. In addition, she would send someone down to the station with it, at no cost to me.

However this was not payola, it was part of the sales package. But later in the show after I had eaten my "free meal" I would rave on and on about how great the food was and encourage people to head to Tee Jaye's and try what I had. This was always good for free coffee after I got off the air. Was that payola? Plugola?

Spook Beckman would say no. Would I have taken huge sums of money to plug someone's products as Alan Freed was accused of doing during the national payola scandals of the 1950's? That is an interesting concept.

So You Want To Be a Rock 'n Roll Star

There was a time when being on the radio really was a payoff for being willing to work for thin pay checks at all hours of the day or night, and in some cases, raggedy radio stations with sub-par facilities.

Being on the air in the 1930's until about the mid 1990's could, and often did make announcers household names and was a way to work in a profession that connected those who were good at it with their communities. It meant something more than just a part-time job, or one that goes away either because of downsizing or frequent ownership changes.

It is not as common today when radio announcers can go anywhere where people have heard of them, or if they have, they are not overly impressed. And for those of us engaging in conversation with anyone who wasn't around when radio was a more mainstream form of entertainment we can't expect them to understand that once upon a time it was a big deal.

One can dial around the radio from FM to AM to XM and Cirius and not find anything as exciting, or as interesting as Wolfman Jack and the style he brought to the industry. Instead, there are a lot of traffic reports, weather reports, sports and when you can find it, music that no longer has much personality, or personalities to make it interesting.

If I were to meet the biggest star on the radio, who ever that is now, I doubt that I would be impressed and I'm sure there wouldn't be any emotional feeling like I had when I met the Wolfman in 1974. Or when I met Kasey Kasem, Dick Clark or any of the other pioneers of Rock & Roll radio.

Even those I never met but admired from afar like Larry Lujack and Charlie Tuna, people like that have never been replaced and never will be. Locally there were many, perhaps the last of this breed being Suzy Waud. WCOL's Terry Tyler, Chuck Martin, Bob Alan, Jack Armstrong, Jerry Gordon, Tom Kennedy, Harry Valentine, Steve Bayliss, Duke Hobson and Mike Mahone, and that stations list could stretch seemingly forever.

WNCI also had its share of both locals and nationally syndicated stars, among them Charlie Pickard, Mike Metzger, Steve Mountjoy, Jack Philips Christopher Paul Tyler, Michael O'Malley, Easy Ed Hayward, Jay Michaels, Mike Raub, E. Karl, Bob North, Dave Anthony and John L. Those are just a few of many.

Over at WCOL-FM names such as Mike Perkins, Neal Martin, Don Gorman, Ginger, Jim Roach, Scoe Benson, Bill Pugh and Terry Wilson were all innovators, and all were different from each other.

This list of once well known radio personalities seems endless when you consider all of the above and count all of the others from WBNS, WTVN, WRFD, WMNI, WBBY, WXGT and all of the other radio stations that are still around, either with the same call letters or with new ones and new configurations. But try to name a half dozen radio personalities now, or even a radio station that has more than just a few announcers on staff. I can barely do that I still pay attention.

Could there be new "Wolfman's" out there waiting to be discovered? Maybe, but would they be worth investing in as the available market shares continue to dwindle? The listeners have scattered to other mediums.

Only the Strong Survive

Within these pages, I have briefly referenced Bob Conners, but how can anyone only briefly reference this guy?

I am a cop by retired trade but I will always be a radio man at heart, so it is unbefitting of me to only tag a paragraph with a mere mention of the undisputed king of radio. Lets face it, Bob is deserving of the very familiar moniker of "Morning Monarch" he's been ahead of the game for decades as the morning voice of 610-WTVN.

He has rarely lost a ratings battle for the listeners that station wants to attract, or for that matter the total number of tuners into period. No other personality can say that.

Even when considering the other legends of Columbus broadcasters, including the likes of past super stars such as Spook Beckman and Doctor Bop just to name two, none lasted as long as "BC." All of us who ever made a living talking into a microphone has to tip our lid's to Bob, and all of us I'm sure are happy to do so.

Energizer Bunny? Please. The rabbit still has miles and years to march if he hopes to last as long.

Beginning around 1965 Bob has been the one constant piece in the WTVN tapestry. To put that in perspective I was an eighth grader at Barrett Junior High School when he started his long journey, and I am old guy now. To further state his longevity, I grew up *after* he got here, became a broadcaster myself, left the business in my thirties and finished a second career as a police officer that lasted two decades.

And to that trivia I can proudly state that as I traveled my own long and winding road I not only knew him, I was once on the same announcing staff at WTVN. In those day's Bob was what he is now; the most listened to guy on the radio.

When I was on the WTVN announcing staff the station had a pretty impressive line up of personalities, including, Dave Logan, Bill Smith, Dave Paar, John Fraim, John Potter and some of the most respected newscasters in the city.

"The Friendly Giant" as it was known then was built around the same guy it still is.

We all knew that Bob was the stations star, and I think we all aspired to be like him. All except Fraim perhaps. John Fraim was in and of himself a star as bright as any, though not nearly as visible in the community or as imitated as BC.

Where John seemed old and stodgy in both voice and appearance to some of us, Bob had that network-like voice and was the best-looking guy in the building.

The closest any of us came to his ability or his presence was Bill Smith, or as I used to kid him, "Junior Bob." Bill was among the most talented personalities in the country who eventually left Columbus for the giant lights of WBZ in Boston.

All of us from that staff came and left, some by choice, others by invitation or mandate, but through all of the changes in not only personnel but type of product WTVN has been, Conners is still the face, if not the voice of Columbus radio.

As a kid who was lucky enough to get my first radio job at WTVN in the early 1970's I was acutely aware of my early fortunes. Any place I went where people knew of my employer I would be reminded, "Oh, you work with Bob Conners?"

Answering yes pumped up my own ego and made me feel if not nearly as important.. At least in the major leagues of radio, and having been afforded that opportunity moving onto other radio jobs seemed easy.

WTVN on a resume was akin to writing it on gold leafed stationary.

I never experienced any difficulty landing good announcing jobs and I landed several.

Bob Conners, after arriving in Columbus more than four decades ago needed to land only one, and he has still got it. Makes my radio career seem somewhat insignificant, but also somewhat special. People still ask when the subject comes up "You worked with Bob Conners?" I doubt that anyone has ever asked *him* if he worked with *me*.

These are among the reasons I traded my headphones for a badge and a firearm. That is not to say that my own nearly twenty years as a broadcaster weren't good ones or that stations didn't get their moneys worth from my efforts, just not as much as the fortunes paid by clients for the right to advertise on the biggest radio show in Columbus history.

If or when he decides to try another career (as I did), two words will suffice, (well done.) Then this guy needs to write a book and tell us all how he pulled it off.

Bob Conners

Standing in the Shadows

I have written about several people who have affected how I approach certain issues. Some employment related, others just everyday occurrences. Various life experiences and some of the reasons I ended up in the circles where I worked and played for the first 50 years of my life.

Some of the stuff in this journal is written for my own index so I will not forget certain things that I want to remember. As I get older I'm finding more and more things that were once vivid memories that seemed to dance around in my head all of the time, but now might require someone saying something that triggers it.

Like when I received an e-mail from someone I had nearly forgotten about. And suddenly my mind was again full of memories about the era and what was going on during it. I am talking about an infamous killing spree that occurred in late 1977 and into 1978 here in Columbus.

The murders became known as, "The .22 Caliber Killings." Central Ohio was gripped with fear as a these serial murders continued for months, seemingly random in nature.

During all of this, I was the overnight DJ at WMNI and it was not uncommon for an occasional weirdo to call into the station late at night and confess to the crimes.

There was even one who did this repeatedly.

After making it known to our PD, Steve Cantrell he advised me to run a tape recorder and to log each call and leave the information for our news director, Martin Petree who was in constant contact with the many law enforcement agencies involved in the investigation. Martin would call them seeking news about the case and in turn would forward to them what we were getting.

On one particular night, the guy who was a repeat caller stayed on the line for several minutes. He sounded intoxicated, and more than a little pissed off, and I had a feeling that he might actually be the killer.

Our technology then was not even close to what it is today but I did what I could to run the tape and call the police. However, by the time I got someone who actually took it seriously the caller had hung up.

I remember this guy asking for the station owner, Bill Mnich. It was two or three in the morning and he wanted the boss's phone number. Of course he didn't get it and I never found out if it was, as it turned out, one of the killers. There were two.

Nevertheless, there was something else about this guy that kept me wondering if it was someone I knew. Perhaps a prankster yanking my chain. He always addressed me by my last name. In addition, he said something about me being just a south end punk. At the time that was not entirely true, I was a little more than that. Moreover, his insight about me was not too alarming because I probably mentioned on the air several times that I grew up on Columbus' south side.

When the case was finally solved and the killers were caught and convicted, they turned out to be two brothers. Gary and Thadeus Lewingdon. The break in the case came when one of them tried to use a credit card belonging to one of the murder victims at the old Woolco store in Great Southern Shopping Center.

Okay there is a south end connection, but I had never known, nor had I ever heard of these guys. And at this time I had no interest in law enforcement and no way of knowing that I would someday not only work in that field, but share office space with many of the investigators on that case.

Several years later, I was hosting a talk show on WCOL and we had booked an author to be a guest on my program. His name was Daniel Keyes. Daniel was promoting his new book, "Unveiling Claudia." It was a non-fictional account of Claudia Yasko who had several years earlier, discussed in great detail facts about some of the .22 caliber killings.

She had been diagnosed as being a person with multiple personalities.

And she did in fact articulate circumstances that only the killer, or someone close to the killer in some of the murders would know.

As the interview with Keyes progressed he mentioned a couple of names of people that I did know, one in particular was Yasco's boyfriend, a guy I knew back junior and senior high school. A punk really who had a pretty tough reputation.

Not long after this program, I left WCOL for a job with the Franklin County Sheriff's Office. My office was across the hall from the detective bureau and as I befriended many of them, I got the opportunity to discuss the .22 caliber investigation. In addition, I learned a few more names that I was familiar with.

It's strange how we walk around not knowing how close we can come to dangerous people or how something, or someone we know turns out to be a chapter in someone's novel. Especially a nonfiction murder mystery.

Silver Bird

One of my favorite stories from WTVN, circa 1973 involved a prized coffee pot that belonged to our morning man, John Fraim. John was the stations star, no doubt about it. The number one morning man in Columbus for years the guy was absolutely spoiled.

When I was the host of the overnight program it was my, or for that matter any jock hosting, responsibility to make sure the studio was prepared for John's arrival at 5:30 AM. This meant having at least an hour of his songs pulled and stacked so he would not have to hunt them.

It meant pulling and stacking the commercials he would need for that first hour, having an updated weather report placed on the console, complete with current weather conditions, ie; the temperature, barometric pressure reading, humidity reading and wind speeds. And finally it was the over night guys job to have a fresh pot of coffee brewing.

The coffee maker was in the men's bathroom. It was the weirdest thing.

The water line to the coffee maker was attached to the toilet's tank. Tick someone off and there might be a possibility that someone would go in the tank instead of the bowl. There were rumors of this nonsense.

But John would not have any part of drinking from the stations complimentary pot. He had his own, and like everything else, John owned it was an exquisite pot.

Probably Sterling Silver, clearly expensive. None of us was permitted to touch it. And John checked for fingerprints to be sure.

One day the pot disappeared and something like an international incident was about to unfold. Memos started flying, some of them outlining the Ohio Revised Code on theft and prosecution. The finger pointing and denials resembled a republican convention. For most of us, it was somewhat funny.

On our message board that held important information such as the EEO guidelines, station licenses and such, someone posted a large note in Bill Smith's hand-writing that said "Bob Conners" stole Fraims' pot."

Bill, perhaps our most talented announcer eventually went to work for Boston's powerhouse radio station, WBZ. He was also our prankster.

I do not remember Bob denying it, or even if anyone was even brave enough to ask him if he knew what had happened to the pot. I wanted it to be Bob; I was in awe of *whoever* did it. I wish I had done it.

A few days past by and the pot was finally located. It was found in the alley behind the Buckeye Federal Building severely damaged from falling sixteen stories.

The sixteenth floor of that building was where our studios were and there was a sort of patio out there where some jocks would go to smoke or just take in the night air.

But no one remembered seeing anyone fling anything over the side, and no one knew how that coffee pot wound up in the alley. Nevertheless, it did fly.

School Days

Our bicentennial year was a strange one for me. Especially on a professional level. In the fall and winter months of that year, I found myself working as an instructor in a broadcasting school. It was another one of those cases where networking with colleagues produced strange results.

I had left "The Friendly Giant" 610-WTVN to pursue this new adventure and it nearly ended my radio career. A friend of mine, who happened to be the Program Director for WBBY-104-FM had introduced me to the schools director as a recommendation to replace him on the school staff. The friend was Robin Goode and the director was a guy I had admired for years when he worked for WNCI, Mike Raub.

Also putting in a good word for me then was another friend who was working at the time for 1460-WBNS, and who was also an instructor at the school, Joe Gallagher, who's real name was Joseph Ucker. Don't say that too loud.

The President and CEO of International broadcasting School was Don Gingerich, who for lack of a better way to say it, was a business maverick. Anyway, I was hired to teach a class of 25, about 23 of them should not have been enrolled. But as was the case in those days if you had about $1400.00 and time to kill you could enroll in just about any broadcasting school in the country.

My own arena for "higher learning" was Career Academy School of Broadcasting. Similar mess.

IBS was located on West 5th Avenue in Grandview in a building that once was home for either a flea market or maybe a revival meeting house, I forget. Whatever it once was, it was a smelly, drafty excuse for a schoolhouse. The heat rarely worked-remember it was winter and the equipment in our studios looked like something that a radio station might have thrown away in the 1940s.

More importantly, our weekly paychecks rarely showed up when they were supposed to. And by the end of the semester, the school locked its doors and moved to Dayton.

Luckily for me I still had a little something going with WRFD and was gearing up for a seven year run with WMNI.   I have lost track of both Robin Goode and Mike Raub through the years, and sadly my friend Joe Gallagher passed away last year.

And aside from two of my students, I have never heard any of the other 23 on the air anywhere.

And I am still not ready to accept any responsibility for that last stat. I had nothing to do with taking advantage of these kids by taking money that should never have exchanged hands. However, I do hope they all found gainful employment in broadcasting.

Who knows maybe some of them ended up in bigger markets and went on to make millions.

And maybe history will record George W. Bush as our greatest president ever, and maybe when you fill your gas tank tomorrow you will be thrilled that gas prices have dropped to 1976 prices overnight. Stranger things have happened.

Hail to the Chiefs

Having enjoyed two careers, both in interesting fields, I have had the opportunity to know and work with some *fascinating* people.

Among some of the brightest minds I have ever worked for were certain radio program directors. E. Karl from WNCI was by far the most outrageous planner of them all. A brilliant Hippie who designed exactly what was right for progressive FM radio in the 1970s. E. was not only a radio *genius*, he was one of the most likeable people I ever knew.

But there were others who poured their collective hearts and minds into making their stations as competitive as possible. All the while serving as mentors to make those of us who worked for them a little better than we would have been if we had not followed their leadership.

Among my favorites were a few from *WTVN*. My first *PD* Jim Lohse I have already discussed. The man who followed him into the role of guiding that great station was John Potter. And, although I was too young and too *immature* to know it at the time, John possessed many of the same qualities had by E. Karl and Jim Lohse.

John and I did not click very well when I worked for him. He was my harshest critic. It seemed I was always in his doghouse. And as a result, I quit. As I said, I was young. For years, I held a grudge against him. However, age and maturity has a way of bringing stupidity into focus. Leaving WTVN over hurt feelings was a huge mistake. I did not get it until years later. But thank God, I eventually got it. As time went along my appreciation for John grew into a friendship that I now cherish.

We do not see each other much, actually at all. However, when we do communicate with each other it is priceless. John Potter is still out there making good things happen in broadcasting. And because of the things he tried to teach me when I was too stubborn to comprehend, I became better at understanding my craft.

Another pretty good boss was Steve Cantrell, WMNIs programmer. Steve was more like one of the guys, but he did keep MNI competitive.

What I liked most about Steve was his acceptance for outrageous behavior. I never ended up in his doghouse. Steve was a master at exploiting country music performers and its listeners. I think he tried to make our product somewhat of a radio version of *TV's* "Hee Haw."

Whatever it was it worked. Listeners to our station seemed to adopt all of the disc *jockeys* into their families. It was not uncommon to show up for work and find presents sent in by listeners.

Then there were three *amazing* PDs at WCOL. First, the guy who hired me-Bob Mitchell. Not at all unlike E. Karl, Bob reminded me of E. in many ways.

He looked like him, he acted like him and he programmed like him. His *mantra* was to create as much fun on the radio as possible. He used to say, "If you aren't having fun then *neither* are the listeners." That made going to work at 'COL a pretty good thing to do.

After Bob left, he was replaced by another passionate broadcaster, Mike Perkins. Mike was a walking thesaurus. His vocabulary was just advanced enough to keep some of us confused and feeling a little uneducated. But Mike could not help it, he was a scholar. In addition, probably one of the most artistic people I have ever known.

Not just with radio ideas, the guy was an artist; he could draw as well as any cartoonist out there. And in the production studio, he was the master. He could make any commercial sound like an exciting saga.

Everything Mike Perkins did was innovative pop-culture.

And the last of my favorite program directors was the man who replaced Mike. Kevin Young. Kevin was a little bit of every *PD* I ever knew. He was likeable yet difficult to understand. His ideas all made sense but not until they grew on you. He had a temper when things went wrong, but somehow was able to make his subordinates get it.

After being balled out by him several times, I got to where I enjoyed it.

Because although I did not always agree with him I somehow knew that he was right.

I Want To Take You Higher

One of the greatest radio stations of all time, as well as one of the oldest in America is still up and doing its thing in Cincinnati, but like most AM stations, it will probably never be the standard of broadcasting that it was. WLW 700 AM.

I have been a radio fan since I was about ten years old. Like many kids in the early 1960s I carried a transistor radio just about everywhere. Including under the covers when I went to bed at night. Back then, Cincinnati seemed thousands of miles away. Later in life it may as well have been a million.

Throughout the 1960s and 70s I was a regular listener to 'LW even as I worked my way through various Columbus Stations. I always hoped that I would one-day work there but it never came to fruition for me. Not for lack of trying. I probably mailed dozens of auditions tapes to "The Big One" as it was known then. I never really knew the exact address, only that their studios were at 9th and Elm. Back in the days before caller I.D.

I would answer every call, hoping against hope that it would be a job offer. The offers did come, but not from the "Biggest One." However, I did make friends with some of the stations iconic names just by calling them to chat and pick their collective minds. These guys were in my opinion the best in the industry. James Francis Patrick O'Neil (JFPO),

Jim LeBarbra, Nick Young, Jockey Joe Kelly, Chris Cage and my all-time favorite, Bob Martin. Rock Stars of radio.

Everything I did in Columbus Radio, every station I worked, I did my best to emulate the guys from 'LW.

I copied their styles, their personalities; I tried to make my show sound like it could have originated from those studios at 9th and Elm in the Queen City. I guess my radio delivery was a form of plagiarism.

Back in 1972 the station had published a book, "Not Just a Sound, the Story of WLW." It coincided with the stations 50th anniversary. I got that book and kept it with me like a Bible hoping that I would derive some sort of inspiration from it, as well as a little fortune, and possibly find a way onto their air staff. It only brought me inspiration.

Nevertheless, I always felt like I did work with these guys even though we were broadcasting 100 miles apart. Because they made listeners feel that way. At least they made this listener feel like that.

What a life they must have enjoyed. Working on a 50, 000 watt *clear channel station, not The Clear Channel company that owns everything between here and Mars, they were owned by AVCO Broadcasting then.

And because of their power and clear channel status, their signal crossed into several states. They were almost a network in themselves. To put it in perspective, when I was at WTVN we were 5000 watts, at WCOL a mere 1000 watts. WLW was the only radio station on the 700 frequency. Anywhere.

And these guys would talk about hitting the bars and nightclubs with their buddies, Johnny Bench, Pete Rose and other ball players from "The Big Red Machine" like it was no big deal.

It was as if they were on par with every sports figure in Cincinnati. I think they were. Guy's like Tom Seaver, Joe Morgan or Tony Perez would stop by the studios to chat for a few minutes and they were treated like anyone else who happened into the room. The WLW jocks seemed larger than them. LeBarbra, aka "The Music Professor" made it sound like he and Sparky Anderson were related.

Life on the radio in a major league sports town. It couldn't have been any better than that. At least I was around to hear it.

You don't mess Around With Jim

The man who gave me my first break in radio in the early 1970's was Jim Lohse. He was the program director for WTVN, then owned by the Taft Broadcasting Company. I have only met one other person who reminds me of Jim and that is the guy who inherited the PD spot when Jim headed south to our sister station, WKRC in Cincinnati. That guy was John Potter. (This is meant as a compliment John!)

Lohse's radio show was called "Lohse's Lounge." I don't really remember that program because he came off the air to assume full time programming duties before I arrived. However, it seemed everyone else in the industry knew it well because every time I mentioned Jim's name someone would say (Lohse's Lounge!) I also never met his wife, but it seemed she too was familiar to everyone else, I think because of her easy to remember name, Lucy Lohse. Jim was famous.

Back in 1973 WTVN had some awesome talent. John Fraim, our morning guy was not especially awesome, but his ratings carried him to the bank each week to make awesome deposits. He was number one in the market.

Either John, or his morning news partner Bill Patterson" was referred to as "The Squire of Pickaway County." I cannot remember which.

Next came our mid-day guy and one of the nicest people in the business, Dave Logan. Dave spent 30 years at WTVN and I think all of them hosting the same mid-day shift. We will probably never see anything like that again. Next, it was the guy everyone called, "Big Gun." Bob Conners *was* that. Following Bob, it was Dave Paar, then, Bill Smith then myself. Potter was our Music Director.

The Friendly Giant. Some of the news talent in that era was Tom Burris, Alan Honigberg, Don Alexander and a few others who I'm not remembering right now.

Anyway, Back to Jim Lohse. In 1973 he wrote a song that was recorded by Al Martino. It was a sugary ballad called "Daddy Lets Play."

A song about a kid begging his father to play with her and the father feeling some guilt about not budgeting enough time for it. Of course we played it endlessly on 610.

Then Jim was the piano player on another song written and sung by our very own Bill Smith. There has never been a better voice or more creative production man than Bill. This guy quickly went into broadcasting orbit when he left Columbus for WBZ in Boston. Anyway, Bill had put together a song called "My Baby Loves To Streak." He put his lyrics to another tune by Charlie Rich called "Behind Closed Doors."

If you can hear that melody in your head sing Bills lyrics which in part are "My baby loves to streak, Lord how she loves to streak-she's always in the nude and I think it's rude......"

The song was released on a record label called No *Wonder Records.* The label itself was pretty cool because it was stamped in a circular pattern that read "It's No wonder it's a hit it's no wonder it's a hit it's no wonder.....you get the idea. We played this record often as well. We had to, Jim was the piano player.

Everyone Jim knew was named "Babe." When he would greet you it was "How ya doin' Babe?" When he had an assignment for you it was "Hey Babe I need you to..." When he was pissed it was, "Now listen here Babe!" All of us could do a Jim Lohse impersonation.

Nevertheless, Lohse was the man. And he let you know it. I have never witnessed a more inflamed temper than his. He did get pissed off a lot. Moreover, he was not shy about it. I still shiver a little when I think about that hot line in the studio. If it rang, Jim was on the other end, and he was not calling to compliment your work.

I found a way into this hard-rocks heart by making him believe that I too believed in ghosts. I am not admitting anything here other than I found a way to keep Jim wanting to keep me around. He was way too into the super natural. Actually, I do not recall having many conversations with the man about anything else. Except when I screwed up on the air.

Sadly, we lost Jim not long after he was sent to Cincinnati. He was discovered in his home with what was reported as a self-inflicted gunshot wound. Another one of those awful moments in my catalogue of memories.

Miracles

WNCI has been an industry leader almost since the birth of that great station. In 1974, WNCI was still in its infancy. A part-time rock station around 1968 with "E. Karl's Incredible Rock Circus" occupying a time slot, and for the most part, the rest of the day simulcasting with its sister station at the time, WRFD-AM 880.

WNCI went on a terror to take over the Columbus radio market. And by the end of the 1970's, it did just that. After WNCI, I think E. went on to become a gazillionaire in broadcasting. To this day, the smartest brain I have ever known.

Not just with radio ideas, but a guy who was more politically astute than most elected officials were at that time. E., short for Eldon, was *brilliant. He was our program director.

* This is not just one man's opinion, if you ever meet anyone who worked for, or who was around this guy, you will probably get the same feedback.

Everyday was a new adventure. E. and another great radio mind, the late Phil Sheridan, who was the stations general manager, gave the staff the most outrageous ideas to work with, that it did not seem like work.

They shared a philosophy that we should make radio so interesting that listeners would not want to turn it off for fear of missing something great. It's format, which fell somewhere between Progressive Rock and Top-40 hits was in and of itself, a radical radio plan.

A few years ago, we lost Phil Sheridan and I will miss a guy who was not only my boss, but also a friend who stayed in touch for nearly 30 years.

Some readers of this text might have known him better as a talented author and theatre historian. Phil published many books on "Those Great Old Theatres" and even managed to help save many of them from demolition in Columbus.

Today's radio listeners cannot appreciate the impact that the medium enjoyed back then. For at that time, there were only 3 commercial television stations to compete with, in terms of broadcasted entertainment, and for a number of years, only WCOL AM and FM to challenge for the rock format on radio.

It was before Columbus had 30 odd choices on the dial, or satellite services that can deliver hundreds of options, before cable TV, CD players, MP3's, I-Pods, mobile phones that deliver TV signals and all of the other options now competing for attention.

Today's programmers and producers have their hands full, as E. Karl predicted in 1974 when he warned those of us who were planning long careers in radio that the future would belong to them. He often spoke of what he envisioned as the coming of cable radio. Some of us thought he was reading too much Buck Rogers!

I have no idea where Eldon Karl Foulk is today, but colleagues in the industry believe that he is somewhere in Europe teaching our neighbors across the pond, new and exciting ways to enjoy whatever form of entertainment they have access to.

I have no doubt that he is revered by many who do not share our language. And I will bet he is having fun with the mess coming out of Washington D.C.-for this truly is a political climate where a guy like E. can light some flares. Wherever he is, he is pissing off someone in elective office. Probably an entire party.

Get a Job

As I continue my journey into the first half century of my life and stop to remember the important people in it, I do on occasion hear from some of them, and so far, all of them who I have are doing well.

Some are still in the professions I shared with them while others have moved into new arenas of living making, still others have joined the ranks of retirement like me. When I was cutting my broadcasting teeth on a microphone at WBUK-FM-96 in the early 1970's I was also working at J-Mart to make ends meet.

J-Mart was a seven store chain in Columbus not unlike K-Mart and I was working nights keeping the floors swept and waxed and the sinks and toilets in the restrooms clean, fresh and sparkling.

While working there I kept the radio plugged into the stores P.A. system and enjoyed the company and music of the areas Rock Stations to help ease the otherwise boredom of being locked in the store alone, all-night. And my usual radio stations of choice in those days were the WCOL stations and WLW-Cincinnati.

I rarely listened to WBUK.

One of the staffers from WCOL-FM back then sent me a nice e-mail one day and in reading his words I was reminded of not only the time I enjoyed hearing him on the radio playing the progressive rock music on

Stereo Rock 92, but when he came back to WCOL in the mid 1980's and became my boss. Mike Perkins is doing well in the Western United States.

For everyone who knew or still knows Mike, and who also knew Eldon Karl Foulk, they will understand when I say these guys are as close as anyone can come to being radio scientists. They were spending their time dissecting the reasons radios were turned on and ways to leave them tuned to their respective stations.

Eldon Foulk, aka E. Karl, was the programming genius working feverishly at WNCI in the early 1970's- Hell bent to overtake the WCOL stations in the Rock Radio wars. Idea guys who when they start articulating their thoughts it is a good thing to have a thesaurus or two on hand.

When it comes to articulating thoughts, be they of praise or criticism, both men have a command of the English language as I have never heard from anyone else. Both could orate better than any language instructor of whose tutelage I was under. Try as I might, Mike would be better able to put that thought into word form than I ever could. As a boss Mike never talked down to us as subordinates, yet anytime I walked out of his office I knew that he had gotten the better of me.

I was fortunate during my tenure at WCOL to have worked with bright program directors who made coming to work something to look forward to. Bob Mitchell who hired me, Mike, Kevin Young and John "The Voice of News" LaPolla.

And something Mike stated in his letter to me that can never be argued by anyone who experienced the-- being paid to do it side of the dial, is that it is unlikely that the radio programmers and managers now will ever work as hard to produce a product, as they do just to survive financially. I think that is what he was telling me. Pass the thesaurus.

It was good to hear from someone who was something of a bookend to my broadcasting career. Someone I listened to and admired at the beginning of it, and someone I worked with and for near the end of it.

Waking Up alone

I still remember the first morning I woke up to find Wes Hopkins gone from WCOL and lying in bed listening to the man who replaced him, and knowing that an era had ended.

That the radio station I had grown up with would never again be as friendly in the morning. J. Parker Antrim was a talented and funny radio personality, and I found myself laughing between the songs as he introduced Columbus radio listeners to his style of morning radio, but somehow I knew that I would miss my old friend, "Mrs. Hopkins' Fat Boy Wes" and his silent, invisible sidekick, "Keemosabe."

I had been listening to and enjoying Wes for a decade, as was every other Columbus radio listener who tuned into 1230 AM for their morning dose of Top-40 hits and corny jokes. And now he was gone.

I was working as a DJ across town at WMNI playing country music at the time but WCOL was still my station of choice because at twenty five years old I had not yet grown out of my preference for rock & roll, and in spite of it's FM challengers, 'COL was a habit that was hard to break.

Listening to Wes Hopkins was a habit impossible to break. Something about his smooth delivery and folksy manner that could calm the trauma of prying ones eyes open in the morning and get ready for what ever the day would bring. He was like caffeine for the soul.

From the days when I was a teenager getting up early to deliver the Columbus Citizen Journal, to getting up for school and later in life for the workday. Wes was always' there.

And as time went along and WCOL would introduce other DJ's in the morning slot I would wonder, whatever became of my friend and could never have imagined that he would one day return to WCOL as an evening DJ, or for that matter, that I would leave WMNI and go to work there and be trained by him.

When I went to work for WCOL in the early 1980's I was told by the program director who hired me, Bob Mitchell to report to the station at 6:00 PM and hook up with Wes who would be showing me the ropes. Nothing Bob could have said could have made me more eager to get started. I adored Wes Hopkins.

What I did not know was that he was planning to leave the station again, and that I was to become his replacement.

I had heard rumors of plans to move him back to the morning show where he belonged but that was not to be. Not long after I signed on he left, but through the years I was able to stay in occasional contact with him by calling and interviewing him from his home in Florida, each time asking him when we could expect another return performance by him on WCOL. Each time he would chuckle and explain those days were over.

And each time he would say that I did not want to believe it. But in 2008 my friend passed away at the age 81.

Throughout this journal I have written other essays of my admiration for this former Columbus broadcasting icon, and how much of an influence he was to my own radio career, and knowing that he is gone changes the way I will listen to morning radio from now on, even though it's been more than thirty years since I woke up hearing him.

Because even though he has not been on the air in decades there was comfort in just knowing that an idol was still around somewhere. As I get older, they are becoming fewer and fewer.

Another important figure from my own youth gone, and each time I get news like this it makes the world around me a little lonelier.

Wes Hopkins

Bryans Song

Having shared a few emotions I have about the passing of Wes Hopkins I was reminded of another guy who is landing at that legendary radio station was easier accomplished than my own hire there.

It took me several years and only the postman knows how many mailed audition tapes and resumes. But Bryan McIntyre began his amazing journey through the WCOL studios and management offices not unlike some others who were able to walk in at the right time and impress someone enough to be hired on the spot.

Bryan was introduced on the overnight show and trained by Mike Adams in April, 1967, the same year Wes Hopkins got on board and the same year I biked around the Southside of Columbus throwing newspapers on porches. No resume, no audition tape, just good chemistry between him and a guy in a position to make it happen, Dan Morris, another long ago station DJ and ultimate Station Manager.

Being tipped off by a college fraternity brother that there was an opening at the station while he was sitting in the Char Bar Grill, Bryan made the wise decision to forego driving his 1957 Ford, electing instead to hop a bus to 22 South Young Street after consuming a few beers to try his luck.

Showing up dressed as most of us did in that era wearing jeans, a sweatshirt, loafers and no socks, he was taken into a studio for a live audition- reading news wire copy, and while "auditioning" Dan called a reference that Bryan had offered from a radio station he had worked for previously in Clarksburg, West Virginia when he was in high school.

The reference must have been glowing enough to land the job, he was hired immediately. Dan Morris, a man who has probably never been accused of making a bad decision in his radio career must have seen the future, Bryan went on to wear many hats with the station, including program director and Operations Manager.

These days whenever his name is brought up, he is remembered as Mr. WCOL. He shared those second floor studios on South Young Street with the best who ever worked in that building. He is as synonymous with the station as Mike Adams, Lou Henry, Jerry Dean, Wes, Bob Harrington, Johnny Hill, Johnny Lane and anyone else who ever introduced rock & roll records there.

Even at the end of WCOL's glory run as the premier rock station in Columbus, Bryan went on to help mold it's sister station, WXGT-92X-FM into the new industry leader with it's switch to Top-40 programming.

I never tire of talking about, or writing vignettes about the old, "New WCOL" gang because these guy's as a collective group were the reasons I aspired to have not only a career in radio, but one that eventually ended in that landmark building at the corner of East Broad Street and South Young Street.

Hail to the Victors

In 1975 WTVN-610-AM was the flagship station for the *Ohio State Buckeyes* and many people thought that was the sole reason the station was number one in the market. I knew better. The station was good, with or without OSU football.

It took a few years to prove that theory; because when 1460 WBNS obtained the rights to OSU games it did little in terms of hurting 'TVNs ratings, they remained #1.

For me, working at 610 in the fall was torturous. We had station I.D. jingles that sounded like the OSU marching band, and almost everywhere in the station there were pictures of Woody, Archie and the other "Gods" of that era, not to mention the mandatory playing of "Hang On Sloopy" by The McCoys almost hourly, and the marching bands version of it in like increments. Yech!

Most of our staff went along with that nonsense whether or not they were actually OSU fans. I couldn't. I worked overnights so it was a little easier to "forget" to say "Go Bucks" every time I opened my microphone. As a matter of fact, many times when it got into the wee hours I would sneak "Hail To The Victors" onto the air and would ignore callers threatening to switch over to WBNS if I didn't play the "Buckeye Battle Cry" or "Hang On Sloopy" a few more times.

Word that there was a DJ in Columbus that openly praised The

Michigan Wolverines reached a jock on a Detroit radio station who happened to be an OSU fan. He called and we bantered about our favorite teams and decided to make a backward bet.

It was customary for people in Columbus to make bets with their counterparts to the North, but usual for someone here to bet against the Bucks. I forget what the bet was, but either I won, or I welched on it because I didn't collect anything from the Motor City, nor did I pay off.

Worse than being an on air pariah because I didn't care for OSU while working for the station that did, and still does have the best Buckeye coverage, was those ridiculous "Beat Michigan dances at Valley Dale.

Can you imagine a "Michigan" fan having to walk on stage in front of thousands of Bucks fans expected to make unflattering remarks about the "Wolves"? It was expected of every WTVN personality. So when it was my turn I came out and said something like, "Are yaw having a good time?"

And as the Buckeye faithful waited for some sort of "Go Bucks" comment they heard something like, "When you leave here tonight, drive safely." I did not get any "Yee Haws" or "Whoo Hoos" shouted back.

Instead, I received a polite applause from about four people.

Things got better for me in autumns to come. When I went to work for WMNI they were the flagship for Notre Dame Football, and the stations owner, William R. Mnich was a graduate from Rio Grande College. We were allowed to ignore the OSU fanfare on Saturdays. So it was fun to exaggerate "*The Game*" over there. The fighting Irish vs. Navy.

Right Back to Where
We Started From

I have written many chapters about "Wild Bill" Bates and his Westerville radio station, WBBY which sadly no longer exist, but during the time it was broadcasting on the 104 FM frequency it was one of the more interesting spot's on the dial. Made interesting by Bates and those who worked there.

Bill Bates was one of the most colorful personalities in the Central Ohio area and because of his broadcasting genius many well known personalities went on to bigger and better careers from their early beginnings in Westerville. I don't know if "better" is the proper way to phrase that because I know they all had to have fun out there. I know I would have, had I had the opportunity to work there for more than one day.

Some great talent that came out of that station and went on to make deep footprints in the local broadcasting landscape.

Among them, one of my all-time favorite radio people, Steve Beekman who I first met when he came to work as a fellow staffer at WMNI in the late 1970's. Then he was known as Stoney Roberts. He and I landed at WCOL together several years later when he was calling himself by another name among the many he has used through his radio travels. He has been known as Steve Scott and Scott McKay among others.

At WCOL he might have been Scott Stevens, the name he went by out at the Bates' DJ camp. Chris Johnston another former WBBY jock and the guy who would later replace me at WTVN, Chris came to 610 at the same time another WBBY jock came over, Mike Motley.

Former WTVN morning man John Fraim had also spent time out there as did former WTVN Sales Manager Jim Pidcock who was known through the years when he was a radio and television voice as Johnny Dollar. Bill Fields, known for his talents at WCOL and WBNS is also on the list. One name that surprised me from the old WBBY days is Dave Phalen.

Dave is the Sheriff of Fairfield County and in all of my years in law enforcement, including ten of them with the Franklin County Sheriff's Office, I never knew that he was a former Disc Jockey. That explains why he is such a smooth interview when matters in Fairfield County draw the interest of the local TV hounds.

Another "perfect" voice who came from the WBBY stable of talent was Scott Kahler. Scott went on to enjoy years of success at WTVN radio.

He was in a small fraternity of benchmark voices that has been highly prized by advertisers through the years like Bill Hamilton, Charlie Pickard and Steve Stratton among the very few. Sadly, Scott passed away in 2008.

Jeffrey Mayfield who once worked out in that Westerville field went on to Billboard Magazine, Rick Seiler and Jay Smith founded their own radio station in Johnstown and one of my all-time favorite DJ's, Denny Erwin who used to do the morning show at WBBY became the "Burger King" by getting into that company's franchise business.

I remember when Denny not only owned and operated his own chain of restaurants; he had his own Burger King bus that went on the road selling the "Whopper." Terri Blair, who later worked at Channel 6 is also an alumnus from the Bates family business.

And two guys I will miss forever, Joe Gallagher and Robb Case who have both passed on in recent years were also among the many talented people who at one time kept the stereo indicator light lit at 103.9 FM.

Joe actually worked opposite me on 1460 WBNS back in the mid

1970's when I was doing late nights on 610 WTVN. And Robb became best know as the helicopter pilot and reporter on "Chopper4" for a number of years, and just months before his passing went on to found his own station, WHKC along with one of his partners who also worked at WBBY, Mark Litton.

Another jock from the WBBY stable was Diane Townsley, believed to be the first female DJ in the area. Yet another 'BBY alum who I once worked with at WNCI, Jack Phillips. Jack and I were at "The Great 98" in 1974.

Readers of the Gary Trudeau comic strip "Doonesbury" know that the mythical radio station in that feature is WBBY. Maybe Trudeau crossed paths with "Wild Bill" at one time or another.

Do It Again

I don't why I liked Damon Sheridan; wait a minute, that's not very nice, I did like Damon, our music director at WNCI more than three decades ago. And later, my program director at WMNI. However, there were times his name was Damien. He had one of those boyish innocent faces and he wasn't a big guy, but he could admonish with the best of them.

When Elton John released the LP - that the song "The Bitch is back" came from it was our "Featured Album of the Week." I do not recall off hand which LP it was, but it was literally on the eve of a time when "bitch" was not an acceptable word for Columbus broadcasting.

I was working late and I did not figure that Damon would be awake so I Cued up TBIB and let it fly. Before the songs long intro ended, the hot line was ringing. It was Damien. I mean Damon. Nevertheless, when I picked up the phone it sounded like the kid from the scary movie. I did not play much of a role in that conversation because Damon did all of the talking, asking among other things if I was trying to get WNCI's license revoked.

He ordered me to lift the needle and play something else. So I complied and dropped it on another cut, right in the middle of the song. That sounded good.

Within a month, TBIB was released as a single and was approved as an acceptable cut and it went on to earn Elton a lot of money. However, my ears still rang every time I played it and I kept my eye on the telephones red light.

About a half dozen years later I was working at WMNI when our PD, Steve Cantrell went off on a sabbatical for awhile to produce concerts and Damon was hired to replace him. I was scared to death to play anything by David Alan Coe for fear of another *Damien appearance.*

I hope Damon Sheridan is still a broadcaster and I hope wherever he is he's doing well. Because when he was not helping me "grow" he was an exciting radio guy to be around.

Soulful Strut

This is about my soulful brothers in Columbus radio. Like my first radio mentor, Beemon J. Black aka "Sugar-Bear" aka Mr. B. and sometimes Kcalb Nosnhoj Nomeeb.

Beemon was Columbus' youngest DJ, 15 years old when he worked for WVKO, and by the time I met him he was a 19-year-old overnight jock at WCOL. Hanging out with BJ as he was known to his posse was a cool thing to do. He knew everyone in the African American community. They were called black guys back then. In fact, B's real name was Johnson.

Even as a white dude I could go in and out of any black circle I wanted, as long as I was with him. Back then, that was not as normal as it is today. I felt like Bobby Kennedy. B. would tell people that I was just very light complected.

After disappearing from Columbus radio for a few years, Beemon re-emerged at WNCI in 1974. He played a helping hand in getting me on board there. However, before I was hired he tried to get me in the door at WVKO. His advice was to approach the station owner, Bert Charles and tell him that I wanted to revolutionize black radio in Columbus by being the only white dude on their air. He suggested I cut an audition tape calling myself Butterball. I never cut that tape, but I did get an interview with Mr. Charles. After laughing at the idea he politely sent me away.

I told this story years later to another friend, former WVKO legend, Bill Moss. Moss thought Mr. Charles had dropped the ball. He thought it would have been cutting edge radio. Those who remember Bill know that he was one of Columbus' most controversial personalities on and off the air.

Especially later in life when he got into politics. So yes, a white DJ called Butterball on a black station appealed to him. I still blow the dust off of Bills local hit record, *"One"* a song he released back in 1969. A song ignored by WCOL but played heavily on WVKO. I miss that station.

I know there is currently a reincarnation of those call letters somewhere on the dial. But it is not the same. Guys like Moss, Kirk Bishop and Les Brown were from a more exciting era.

Another elder statesman I miss from the Old WVKO is Eddie Saunders. Eddie was probably the biggest name in Columbus radio. Bigger than Spook Beckman and Doctor Bop in many ways. I think he continued on the air well into his '70s.

When I think back to the issues of racial unrest that existed in certain Columbus neighborhoods as recently as the late '60s and early 1970s, I know that radio and the people in it weren't much a part of it. If I can say it, there was a sort of "brotherhood". (Sorry, too easy.)

Music appreciation has a way of mixing us. And by the way, if you scroll back and look at the many names Beemon went by, the one that is hardest to pronounce was his name spelled backward. He used that one to confuse telemarketers and bill collectors.

And, as Beemon would say at the close of all of his programs, "Remember they can't take away our music so keep on truckin'."

Fever

F ans of the 1970s sitcom "WKRP in Cincinnati" might remember
that the producers of the show did in fact loosely base it on a real
life radio station in the Queen City with similar call-letters.

WKRC in Cincy was, and may still be WTVNs sister station.
Moreover, when the planning for the comedy show began the writers
and producers explored WKRC and picked their brains for ideas that
could resemble realism. Actually, when all of this was going on, former
WTVN programmer-Jim Lohse was the PD at WKRC.

On the TV show the character of WKRPs program director, Andy
Travis did sort of remind some of us of Lohse. As some of the others on
the show reminded us of people we knew. Mr. Carlson was like some
General Managers all of us have known.

No disrespect to the news directors I worked with, but Les Nesman
reminded me of a few here in Columbus. Herb Tarlik was a carbon copy
of every salesman I ever knew, Venus Flytrap had common personality
traits of the soul brothers working the Columbus airwaves and every
station had a few hotties like Bailey Quarters and Jennifer Marlowe.

But I only knew one guy who could hold a candle to Johnny Fever. I
was working nights at WMNI. I walked into the vestibule one night on
my way into the studio and noticed this guy who appeared to be in his

early 40s, long salt and pepper hair, scraggly whiskers and a well-worn t-shirt with some sort of rock n' roll logo on it.

The guy was asleep on the couch. Snoring. In addition, there was a brown paper sack on the floor that contained what appeared to be his worldly possessions. My first thought was that someone had forgotten to lock the door and perhaps a homeless man had wandered in.

I thought about calling the police to have him escorted out. Instead I woke him and asked if he was lost or confused or if there was something I could do to help him out.

He asked if my name was Rick. He explained that he was the new guy and he was waiting for me to train him. My program director did leave me a memo on this but I made it a habit of checking my mailbox at the end of my shift. That gave me an excuse to argue new policies and such.

Anyway, we got things worked out and I quickly learned this guy needed no training. He was about the best disk jockey I had ever heard.

In fact, he turned out to be someone I idolized as a kid. He had worked at WCOL back in its heyday and had a voice and personality that was truly amazing. His name was Jim Davis. Jim was not only tremendous on the air, he was amazingly funny off the air. His off air persona was a mirrors reflection of Doctor Johnny Fever.

He dressed like him, had similar sarcasm and a track record in the business that included gigs at stations from coast to coast. A rocker from the old school stuck in Columbus. And like the character on WKRP Jim hated rules. He broke them all.

I remember sitting in a DJ meeting after the PD had finished a rant and rave about guys not following the format, and when he asked if there were any questions we all looked around the room and broke into laughter. Jim was asleep. Someone nudged him and he farted. He was the best.

Another fond memory was a contest idea that our PD had come up with. It was called "Make-It-Or-Break-It." The idea was for Jim to play two new songs and allow listeners to call in and vote on which song should be added to our play list. Jim would play the songs then let the phones ring off the hook without answering them.

After a few minutes, he would come on the air and break the loser. He would smash it on the table and play glass-breaking sound effects and tell the listeners that they voted it the loser. What was really going on was Jim was the only voter. One time he smashed a George Jones record and declared an obscure song recorded by an unknown artist that sounded like crap the winner.

The Jones record went on to become a smash hit. Jim's winner was in the trash when the PD showed up the next day. Because of his talents and likeability on the air, women were always coming to the station late at night to meet him. However, he usually ignored the attention unless one showed up that was hard to look at or smelled bad, Jim would greet them at the door and tell them that his name was Bill Weber.

Bill was our morning man. He would tell them that Jim went home sick.

I could do this all night. I loved that guy.

Another one of those Gems that rarely comes along in life. Fun to listen to and fun to just hang out with and observe. And as was his history, he didn't stick around long.

Sometimes chasing jobs that paid more money, Jim left us after about a year.

But he left enough memories behind to keep those of us who knew him laughing for years to come..

Norman

When I sit down in front of this key board and ponder what needs written I simply think of something, or someone on my mind and try to craft a bunch of words that will hopefully tell some sort of story.

Sometimes listening to old tape recordings of various radio shows and different Disk Jockeys I have known through the years gives me such inspiration. I came across a tape of Scott Norman, a WCOL DJ from 1984. Scott was one of the last in a long line of talented WCOL morning jocks before the station morphed into its first go around as a Talk Radio station.

Carrying on the tradition of guys before him like J. Parker Antrim, Wes Hopkins and Johnny Hill, he was a funny guy. But like so many others, Scott did not stick around long enough, and when he left, I replaced him on the morning show for a brief period. Back when radio was fun to listen to stations did not need "teams" of announcer's to get the listener's up in the morning.

No zoos or crews, just a friendly voice who had a knack for bantering about the weather on it's way or the overnight developments that morning risers might find interesting, and of course someone to keep time and offer a little commentary about the music they were playing.

Even I could do that.

Another tape I came across had a couple of WMNI DJ's I worked with, Joe Maxwell and Mike Taylor. A couple of young guys who also did not stick around long enough. On the tape, I am heard interrupting Maxwell's show by introducing him to a new pup that I had gotten that day. Joe is asking what my new Boxer's name was and I am explaining to him that I named him "Stargell" after my favorite baseball player.

Joe remarked that the dog did resemble Willy Stargell and I'm asking if it is because of the round black face or the stout Brown body, and after a long pause he says, "Okay, you probably just got us both fired." Priceless.

On the same tape Mike Taylor is saying goodbye for the night and introducing my show coming up next, he then starts his next record on the wrong speed and tries to shift the gear lever to set it on the correct speed and somehow knocks the tone arm off the record. It was a beautiful moment.

Through the years, I have kept many tapes of people I have worked with and still get a kick out of listening to and remembering a time when life was simpler. And as I listen to this stuff, I am reminded that back then it seemed like time stood still, that I could never have imagined this far into the future, or that I would actually live as long as I have.

I was in my twenties, everyone who was ever important to me was still alive and I was taking for granted the belief that they always would be.

Thinking of people in their forties as old, that my kids would always be kids and that I could bluff my way through one radio station to another, break some rules along the way and chase dreams at a casual pace. Time can really be a bastard.

Thankfully, I preserved enough of the era by stopping to thread a tape and remembering to take it with me when I left the station. Those voices on the tapes now are older now, and in all likelihood feel a little like I do.

Wondering where the time went, where our colleagues from that time ended up or how many of them are no longer on the planet. What I would not give to be able to feel twenty-something again, if only for a few minutes.

Reunited

In the summer of 2003, I attended the third annual WCOL reunion that was held at "Broadcast Lake" on Dublin Road before the station moved to its current location on West 5th Avenue. About eighty former WCOL staffers showed up for the gala, many had traveled here from different parts of the country just to attend this special event.

So many people I grew up listening to, guys like Mike Adams, Johnny Lane, Brian McIntyre, Dave Bishop, Roger Hornung and a continued list of who's who from the Columbus radio history pages.

The Saturday night party was broadcasted live on the 1230 frequency and all of us got the opportunity to recount a special memory from our time at Columbus' most legendary station. The weather for the outside event was perfect, the food and drink was plentiful and the camaraderie was unbelievable.

Staffers from as far back as 1953 through those of us who were there in the early 1980s came together as if we had all been friends for years.

One of my favorite stories that night came from Bob Harrington. He had come to WCOL from a station in Florida in the mid '60s and was actually hired during his interview and went on the air about a half hour after the interview. Bob told many wonderful stories but best was when in 1965 he was asked to pick up Diana Ross and the Supremes at the airport for a concert appearance here.

He had a GTO convertible and when he picked the girls up he decided to put the top down to impress them. As he drove them to their hotel, the wind all but destroyed their beehive hair-do.

Johnny Lane and Mike Adams articulated stories about the "Battle of the Bands" at the Ohio State Fair. One of them would be on the phone talking to the DJ on the air about the huge crowds lining up to get in and there wasn't anyone there. Moreover, sometimes the jock calling in was actually inside the WCOL studios when he called in.

Neal Martin who will always be remembered for saying the "F" word on the air, and who was ribbed about it told a story of when WCOL was at the zoo a male kangaroo attacked him because the animal thought he was too close to a female kangaroo.

Tip Carpenter, the stations engineering guru for several decades recanted a time when an irate business executive in a suit was entering the 'COL lobby when a big wind gust came along and blew the water from an awning and drenched him. When he went inside he asked the receptionist, former WBNS TV anchor-woman Dana Tyler- "Who's responsible for this?" Dana replied, "God I guess." Dana had come to the party from New York City where she anchors the evening news for the CBS station there.

My own story was of a time back in 1965 when I had won a prize from WCOL and when I went to the station to get it I met Mike Adams, and later in life while working at 'COL I interviewed Mike on the air from his home in California where he is a professor at San Jose State.

All of this program can still be heard by logging on to the 1230 WCOL Fun Pages" and clicking on the link for the "Third Annual Reunion" and you can peruse some cool photos from not only that night, but from WCOL's past on "Mikeadams.org."

Cover of the Rolling Stone

I was reviewing the May 10, 1971 issue of the WNCI "record rap", a weekly survey of the top fifty songs in Columbus and distributed exclusively in Lazarus record departments back "yon" and because I hadn't seen one in decades, I was excited just to be holding a copy of "record rap", its title in lower case letters as it were was NCI's bigger and better version of the "New WCOL" Hit Line Surveys also available at Lazarus.

Where the 'COL list was a two sided piece of paper about the size of a standard letter-envelope the 'NCI offering was an 8x10 four-sided fold-out offering not just the list of top songs of the week, but photos of the rock stars' of the day, bio's, programming notes and a weekly comic strip imagined and drawn by the stations' incredible program director, E. Karl. Remember "E. Karl's Incredible Rock and Roll Circus?"

It was the launching pad for WNCI's future as a rock station and to that point makes E. to WNCI what Doctor Bop was to WCOL. By the way, the comic strip was called "The Incredible World of E. Karl,"** There is that word again!

I wish I had kept the "R R's" from all of those decades ago, if I had I would own an incredible source of early and mid 1970's rock & roll history, not to mention the keepsake value of having known and worked with some pretty good people.

The late "Brother" Dave Anthony wrote a weekly column for the "Rap" called "Dave Anthony & All That Jazz" which was also the title of his weekly Jazz-Blues weekend show that he hosted in addition to his daily 5-8PM regular rock program.

I would compare Dave's on-air delivery to something like a Morgan Freeman narration. Laid back, smooth and in no way in a hurry, Dave was as cool off the air as he was on.

At a time when WNCI was fighting its guts out for the top radio rung held by WCOL and its screaming high-energy DJs, there was Dave, taking it easy, but playing the exact same catalogue of tunes.

The "Record Raps" I am again in possession of, "I have two-the May 10, '71 issue and January 17, 1974 compliments of another old friend in that company, Mike Eiland. Mike has been not only in this area for decades, but like only a fortunate few he has managed to stay with the big guns, WTVN and the other Clear Channel sibling's since before I was shaving.

As I was perusing these rare collector issues I was remembering a song recorded in 1974 when I was a DJ at WNCI called "Cover Of The Record Rap," a parody attempt of the Dr. Hook Classic, "Cover Of The Rolling Stone." Myself and another jock had put together a musical fantasy explaining how our lives and our careers would not be complete until we got our pictures on the cover of the "rap."

The song was not allowed to be played on the air, but somehow it was a few times very, very late at night. My part was great; I was actually a veteran singer having sung in my earlier life for the Barrett Junior High School Glee Club.

My solo version of "Kumbaya" is breath taking and usually brings tears to my own eyes and my ego when articulating my many "gifts" explodes in lavish colors and vibrating sound when I get on a roll. To some that earlier training might have been missed but to me I was just a tad shy of amazing.

A candidate for the fifth Beatles slot.

What's Your Name?

B anks, News and Shoes. Radio station call letters once actually stood for something as opposed to merely being three letters that are designed to express something. Keep in mind that first one, always a "W" on this side of the country, except of course for Pittsburgh's KDKA which was grandfathered before this distinction was outlined.

Locally some were pretty cool. WCOL kind of speaks for itself. And as an old WNCI promo used to announce, "The N is for Nationwide. It was Nationwide Communications Incorporated back when the insurance giant owned it. Another of my alma maters, WRFD was Rural Farm Delivery. It was a station owned by the farm bureau.

WMNI was named after the stations founder, William R. Mnich. The first three letters of the family's last name. In fact, what is now called "The Rock" was once called WRMZ. The "Old Mans" initials. And I say that in a respectful way. "The Old Man" was what every station manager was called back in the day. And later WRMZ became WMGG. See the pattern?

WTVN was WHKC renamed. It may have had something to do with its affiliation with what was then called WTVN-TV-now called WSYX.

WOSU. Hmm, I wonder.

WCBE stands for Columbus Board of Education and my favorite

was WBNS. Banks, News and Shoes. For as long as I can remember it has been owned by the Wolfe Family, printers of the Columbus Dispatch and owners of other news sources. I understand the books and news reference, but I have always been puzzled by the shoes.

WBBY which used to occupy a spot around 104 on the FM band was owned and operated by Bill Bates. Another interesting radio name is an old one returned, the resurrection of WTVN's old name, WHKC. Now an FM station and co-founded by the late channel 4 chopper pilot and news reporter, Robb Case.

When I first Robb he was a kid in high school. He was a DJ for USA Roller Skating Rink and our station, WNCI was there for what else, "WNCI Night." Robb was one of those hip dudes who gave us a crash course on public performance. The "kid" had the live-DJ thing down to a science.

The story behind the WHKC call letters is they are his spouses' initials. Chivalry lives. But then that is how I remember Robb Case. Sadly he is another friend who passed away too young. We lost him a few years ago.

Judy in Disguise

SkyLucy? That is how Fred Beckman knew Casper the Camel and Spook is what we called Fred. It gets confusing. Changing names in the broadcasting business kept many personalities from needing to have unlisted phone numbers. As host of my first radio show on WBUK-FM-96 I was known simply as R. Dean. I took that cue from a few of my favorites from that era over at WNCI, E. Karl and John L.

Mike O'Malley could not be found in the phone book but Mike Alerdice might have been there. Who would have guessed that WTVN's Dave Logan would really be David Grueser? How about Joe Ucker who was better known as Joe Gallagher.

Mike Adams came to WCOL from Norwalk, Ohio where he was born Mike Hackney. Fellow 'COL staffer Neal Shapiro preferred to be known as Neal Martin.

Although I think there was probably more to 92X's "Baltazar" and "Geronimo" I never knew for sure.

One of my favorites was Steve Beekman from WCOL-WMNI-WBBY and probably a hundred others on the country's radio logs. Steve changed names every time he changed employment. Among his best was Stoney Roberts at WMNI. WCOL's Johnny Lane was Johnny Lankenau and Dave Bishop is Dave Daugherty.

WCOL's "Godfather" Doctor Bop was Hoyt Locke.

Nevertheless, many did throw caution to the wind and brave the open world of radio by sticking to what their parents gave them. Although some liked to think that Suzy Waud was a lounge-in-cheek moniker, Waud was her name.

Here are some pretty cool names that went on as is. Pam Easterday from WMNI. Joe Carfagna from WTVN. Vance Dillard also from '610.

Carl Wendelken from WMNI. In the mid 1960's WCOL had a guy named Jim Hazeltine, in the '70s I worked with Paul Fertig at WBUK

And then there were those guys with natural show biz names like Wes Hopkins and Brian McIntyre from WCOL. Bob Conners, Dave Paar, John Fraim, Steve Stratton and Bill Smith all from 610-WTVN. Jack Evans and Dick Zipf from WBNS-Yeh Boy! These are just a few examples of who was really who on the Columbus air waves.

Ramblin' Man

If you search the archives of this journal and find my piece titled, "Take This Job and Shove It" I gave an insight of what it was like for me to welcome Johnny Paycheck to the Ohio State Fair in 1978 while working as a DJ for WMNI. Pretty much a disaster in front of more than 80,000 country music fans when Paycheck coughed up a little vomit after arriving on stage several minutes late.

However, the following year when I was sent to introduce Waylon Jennings on the same stage I experienced a day I will be forever thankful for a number of reasons. Not least among them I got to not only see the greatest country singer ever, up close and personal, I got to spend time with him.

More special even now that he has passed away. Meeting Waylon ranks right up there, just ahead of meeting Johnny Cash the following day. Two super-stars who make today's country giants look very, very small.

When Waylon stepped out front to perform he had his tremendous rock band, "The Waylors" behind him, and as an added bonus, members of Buddy Holly's "Crickets" sitting in for an unbelievable Holly-medley.

I stated that his group was a rock band because that is exactly what they were. Even though Waylon was in his prime on the country charts in the late '70's-his live performances rivaled those of any "rock" group of the era. They were loud, fast and driven hard, just like their front man.

"Ole Waylon" was labeled an outlaw in the mid '70's by the power structure in Nashville because of his unwillingness to have his brand of music tampered with to conform with the more traditional country "twang" and because he insisted on making it his way.

He didn't buy into the glitz of the Country Music Association and their silly awards programs, he stopped greasing his hair and slicking it back, opting instead to wear it long and unkempt, he grew a beard dressed like Jesse James and took his act back to Texas to develop what today's country artists are still *trying* to play.

His "Outlaws" album in the mid-'70's with Willie, Tompall Glazer and Jesse Coulter is still regarded by many as the greatest country album of all time.

Downtown

In 1947, WCOL moved into a new three-story building at 22 South Young Street, just down the street from where they began in 1922 as WMAN, located in the Broad Street Baptist Church at 583 East Broad Street. The church owned the station in the beginning. Radio by the way, first became a reality that year, making WCOL one of the oldest stations in the world.

Sometime before 1929 they had studios on South High Street for a period, and in '29 they moved to the old Seneca Hotel at Broad and Grant. It was while they broadcasted from the Seneca that the call letters were changed to WSEN. Later in the 1930's after the call letters had been changed to WCOL the station was owned by the Wolfe Family, who also owned WBNS.

When laws were changed restricting ownership of more than one station in the same market the Wolfe's opted to sell WCOL and keep WBNS because it had a more powerful signal. I wonder if the Wolfe's ever regretted that decision.

Someone in the family probably did by the mid 1960's when WCOL was the undisputed ratings leader in the Columbus market. And still today, WCOL-FM is usually in the top two. While both WBNS stations are lucky to be in the top ten. And by the way, the Wolfe family still owns the "BNS stations.

What a time that must have been back in 1947 when WCOL moved into their new digs. A few years after the war, the U.S. economy kicking into high gear, major events unfolding across the country. Truman becomes the President, Henry Ford dies, Drive-In movie Theatres are introduced, the country is changing and so is radio.

Think about it, although television had been recently invented, few people had a TV set. Radio was the media king. In addition, the personalities who worked for the city's top stations, WCOL among them were household names in just about every house.

Those of us who came later cannot know how special those people were. We can only hear the stories and wish we had been among them.

When I worked at WCOL the studios were still at 22 South Young Street, which was the address for the main entrance. But it fronted Broad Street at 195. I used to sit in those studios and speculate about what life might have been like back in '47 both inside that building and outside on the street. I have always been fascinated by that decade anyway so I could craft some pretty vivid mental pictures.

I could visualize a huge WCOL staff, because in those days it required many people to both operate a radio station, and to create the entertainment. The business was still in the era of *some* radio drama programming and some live house musicians. I know from actual photographs the ceilings were much higher for acoustic purposes, and there were more prominent glass walls separating sound rooms from broadcast booths.

They had in-house producers, directors and writers as well as performers. News, especially local news played a much bigger role than it did by the time the station started rocking in the '60's. And, because it was the dominant media in that time all stations were more closely monitored for content than they became in later years. It was a far more serious, and important business than what it had become by the time I started in the early 1970's.

I can imagine the vehicles parked along that corner in 1947. Keeping in mind that most of them were probably models built in the 20's and 30's.

And the listeners themselves. Just think of the famous names of the era and how many of them either passed through, or lived in Columbus and probably listened to that station. There is a lot of history associated with WCOL and almost everyone I have ever talked to who was in this area before my time remembers something, or someone associated with it.

The building itself is still there. If you visit, stand in front of the 22 South Young entrance and look up to the top of the building. The huge WCOL call letters are still engraved in the concrete. At least that has not been tampered with.

Part of the first floor has been shamefully turned into a Subway sandwich shop, and the rest of what was once a beautiful Columbus landmark appears nearly vacant, but is sparsely leased for office space.

The building should be purchased by the City of Columbus. It should be restored to its 1947 grandeur and turned into a Columbus broadcasting museum. Picture the exterior entrance's and the canopy's over them framed in chrome and neon signage on the side of the building. (Familiar building accents in downtown Columbus in that era.)

Preserving the floor in the lobby with the WCOL logo inlaid into the tiles. (Most of that is still there). Rebuilding the huge auditorium-like studios and installing period broadcast equipment. They are doing something similar over at the Lincoln Theatre on Mt. Vernon Avenue to celebrate our city's entertainment past. Why not leave something else good behind for future generations to enjoy?

WOLD

Harry Chapin's 1973 song, WOLD is probably a favorite among many DJ's of that era. I know I played the hell out of it at WNCI. Harry really captured the emotion of life on the radio with that one. And as time went along in my own career I met many guy's who could sing "Feelin' all of 45, goin' on 15." A true Van Gogh pressed in vinyl.

It could have been worse, I could have related to his song, "Taxi." Not that there is anything wrong with that career, but I would not have been any good at it. I get lost when I travel north of Broad Street.

I was fortunate to have had the many wonderful AM and FM opportunities I enjoyed, but I never experienced moving away from the familiar surroundings of Columbus as did many of my colleagues. I almost did a few times.

For myself, as I am sure was true for many, I used to fantasize about working at such powerhouses as WLS in Chicago and CKLW a little further North into Canada, and every time either would run a job opening in Billboard Magazine I would fire off a T&R. I never got responses from anyone that big, but I did get a few from other markets.

I used to test my own marketability a lot back then. I'd scan the ads for job openings and send out tapes and resumes to places I had no intention of ever going to just to see if I could get a response.

And I did get some. I could have ended up in Plainfield, Vermont, Hartford, Connecticut, and Cutbank, Montana among a few I can remember. The Hartford job would have at least put me in the New York market. It was just across the Long Island Sound.

Nevertheless, here I stayed. Probably out of fear of the unknown. Or maybe because the jobs I already had were pretty good. But as I wrote in an essay last month, had I gotten a call from WLW I would have packed my tent and headed south.

Which makes me wonder-When my radio career was over; could I have hooked up with Hamilton County Sheriff Simon Lees and worked as his PIO?

Detroit City

A sk young radio announcers today if they have a broadcasting license and they might think you are putting them on. I am just getting over finding out ten years ago that they were available then for thirty bucks and a signed application.

And don't you hate it when we old dudes begin a thought with, "In my day....?"

It is hipper now to say, "Back in the day...." a license was required and they were not easily earned. When I first went after my Third Class License with "Broadcast endorsement" the "endorsement" word here is key because without it you could not legally record transmitter readings onto a log, it became another of my many quests ending like a bad dream.

In those days, there was a three-part test that you had to take from the licensing codebook. Elements one and two were simple, they were just about the laws governing broadcasting, but the third requirement fell under element nine. The hardest math test ever designed for persons like me who did not pay enough attention in algebra class. And forget calculators, they were not around yet.

The eight-hour test had to be taken at an office of the Federal Communications Commission. The closet one to Columbus was in Cincinnati and since they had seasonal scheduling at the time I needed to be licensed, I had to make tracks for Detroit, Michigan, the next closet testing location. Moreover, the tracks I made were in a snowstorm. 188 miles worth.

When I got close to the Motor City, I nearly detoured into something called "Tunnel to Canada" by coming close to missing an exit. I dodged a bullet on that one. Next, because I had not thoroughly planned the trip out, I arrived in Detroit around 5:30 in the morning. The test was not scheduled until 9:00.

Therefore, my traveling mate and I had to find somewhere safe to huddle for a few hours. Not to offend the good people of Detroit, but we found it to be the dirtiest, most frightening environment either of us had ever seen.

It was cold and nasty and there I was in the downtown area with a girlfriend, Patti, who would later in life give birth to my second son Kevin, with only a little money and no plan except to take a test when the Federal Building opened. We landed in some hole-in-the-wall of a restaurant to wait. Whatever I ate made me sick, it was the kind of sickness no one wants to know about.

The morning was not going well at all.

I should have spotted the omens and turned my 1969 Plymouth Fury around and headed south at this point but instead I made it to the FCC for my test. After breezing through the first two elements I began answering the questions in the final phase. Sheer terror began to consume my concentration.

Scarier than downtown Detroit at 5:30 in the morning.

It was all in some horrible math language that I had never seen before, or if I had, I had forgotten. At the end of the day when the tests had been graded and the administrator revealed that I had failed I really felt like a failure. Hmm. I was told that I would have to wait two more months to be eligible to retake it.

I don't know who had a worse day, me or my girlfriend who had to wait somewhere in the building all day while I was wasting my time doing something I obviously was not prepared to do.

Worse than knowing I failed, I had to tell her that the entire miserable experience was a complete waste of time. So I lied to her. (What?) I told her that I would not get the results for a few weeks. I did not want her trip home to be as long as mine was going to be. Besides, I was embarrassed. In addition, to add to my misery she kept saying, "Don't worry, I'm sure you did fine."

I did pass the thing and was awarded a license on my next attempt and when I got it-, it was a piece of paper not much larger than a standard envelope. I displayed it in a 16 X 24 inch frame. I earned that miserable *requirement.* These days it lives folded in an old scrapbook.

And now, to know that because of advanced technology and the ability of transmitters to record their own Friggin readings I am truly amazed. Among other repressed emotions from many decades ago.

Walk On the Wild Side

Spook Beckman, like Wes Hopkins was in a league by himself. Where Wes was best known by the teens and young adults of the 1960's and '70s, Spooky was known by generations of radio listeners. I first got the opportunity to work with him in the mid '70s when Spook was in the middle of his radio comeback after being away from the business for a while. It was at WRFD.

The station had a format of mostly Adult Contemporary music but the Spook was given free reign to play what he wanted. Mostly standards and Big Band music. Disco music was just getting its foot in the door elsewhere and Spook had his own ideas about doing a live "Disco" show with a live audience.

He worked out a deal with a Grove City bar inside what was then Howard Johnson's- called "The Post Time Lounge" to appear on Friday and Saturday nights with what he billed as "Spook Beckman's Disco Daddy Show." He had a specially made pajama-type outfit that spelled that out across the back, and for me, his music guy, a T-shirt with the same logo. (My job was to play the records while Spook mingled with the crowd telling nightclub jokes and sharing drinks with them.)

People coming to the show hoping to hear Disco tunes were serenaded by Al Martino, Buddy Rich and Patti Page records. Spook hated Disco music. However, it was his brand of the genre and his loyal fans never complained. They were there to see Spook Beckman. They would have come if there wasn't any music.

There was this one "gal" named Ginger who used to call Spook several times a day at the station and pester him. "She" was absolutely in love with him. She offered him the moon and back again. A sultry voice that had us all fooled.

Bill Stewart, one of the funniest radio personalities I have ever worked with voiced a little jealousy about this caller. Bill seemed to know more about her than the rest of us. I always believed that he was behind Gingers obsession with Spook. He was probably the only one on the staff that "knew" Ginger was a man. Or was she? He.

One night Ginger made good on her promise to show up at "*The Post Time Club*" *in Grove City to meet the Spook*. Spook Beckman was a large man, Ginger was bigger. Hair like Dolly Parton that may very well have been her own, a chest bigger than Dolly's, that might also have been her very own, and make-up that would make Tammy Faye envious.

Someone had passed me a note up on stage that she was sitting alone at a corner table and drinking entirely too many cocktails. In addition, Spook, who could also consume more alcohol at these shows than most men half his age had no idea she was there.

It was a feature of the program that audience members would request something special and Spook would do his best to dance with them.

When I read Gingers note I announced that we had a special request from the lady in the corner and when Spook looked over at her he whispered to me, "There is no way." He looked again and whispered, "I ain't that damn drunk."

When I told him that it was Ginger he nearly fell off the stage laughing. And being the showman he was he met her on the dance floor and did one of those no-touching dances. It was like the *Twist meets the Conga*.

At the end of the night Spook kept me going in and out of the parking lot to make sure she was not out there waiting for him. He was afraid to leave. He had had more than a few drinks and he kept asking, "That was a man wasn't it?"

No one knew for sure. Except maybe Bill Stewart.

Spook Beckman

You Should Be Dancing

B ack in the late 1970's while working as a DJ for WMNI radio, a management decision was made to turn WMNI-FM into an all Disco station, but keep the AM side of the business Country. How is that for contrast?

The FM call letters were changed to WRMZ. The stations mascot was a Zebra and our logo became Z-100. This was in the days before exact digital identification. (I never did get the connection between striped horses and dance music.) It was easier in those days. WCOL-FM was Stereo Rock 92, WNCI was the great 98 and so on.

In the brief history of its Disco format WRMZ was actually a pretty good radio station. Of course you had to like that genre of music, but overall we did do it right. Here we were, a bunch of cowboys familiar mostly with the music of George Jones and Tammy Wynette, sneaking up on the FM pop stations with The Bee Gees and Patrick Hernandez records.

We developed a good following quickly but for whatever reasons, we did not stick with it long enough. Of course the Disco era itself didn't last very long, but from that hip sound- WRMZ could have evolved into whatever pop-related format it wanted to. Management decided on Easy Listening, Or as it was called in those day's, Elevator Music.

That lasted for a number of years and eventually an oldies station, named WMGG (Still the William Mnich initials) was born. And it was a very good sounding radio station. But as is the usual case for "Oldies" oriented radio stations, it too eventually became something else.

Still owned by the Mnich family and doing better than it did in previous incarnations with its hard edge rock format. It seems to have found its niche. During its brief tenure as WMGG I was invited to return for a brief radio stint as a weekend DJ, but by that time I was deep into my law enforcement career and could not give my little program the attention it would have required to make it successful.

Besides, I had grown too old, or had matured beyond being able to tolerate temper tantrums from gung ho Program Directors. And WMGG had one of those. I really think his hobby was playing with the telephone because he kept our in-studio "hot-line" ringing off the hook. Going into a tailspin if he heard even the slightest deviation from his carefully planned play-list.

Play "Fun Fun Fun" instead of "I get around"? Threats of being fired could follow that bit of insurrection. He called himself Steve Edwards in those days and in the early 1970's he was WNCI's Steve Mountjoy. One of the best radio announcers I ever heard, just not my favorite boss.

It was because of that I left the station. I just could not show up on Sunday nights for a five-hour radio show and continue to be ordered into the PD's office every Monday morning for such infractions as playing the wrong jingle or the wrong Elvis record. "Hound Dog" instead of "Jail House Rock?" How could I have been so bold!

I Was Kaiser Bill's Batman

I have written many stories about my good friend from Boston who worked at 610 WTVN back in the early and mid 1970's. Bill Smith was the most talented person I ever met in radio. When I say that he was my old friend I am echoing what everyone who knew him might say. I have never spoken to anyone who ever had something negative to say about him.

Bill made a lot of us younger DJ's glad to be working at WTVN and he made a lot of us better talents. In a business that can be cutthroat and back stabbing because of clouded egos his willingness to rub off on others was exceptional. Exceptional because here was this guy, not much older than me but clearly one of the best on any station, radio or television.

Moreover, this was a time when WTVN was saturated with heavy hitters.

Bob Conners, John Fraim, Dave Logan, John Potter and Dave Paar among them. With apologies to them all, Bill was in a league of his own. Nothing phony, just God given natural talent that seemed to explode all around him.

My best memory of working with him was my final night at WTVN before I left for a spot at WNCI. Bill and his constant companion in those days, a girl named Linda had put together a "modest" going away party for me. Just the three of us.

My shift didn't end till 2:00 AM on WTVN-FM-96, but Bill's show on 610 AM was over at 10:00PM and during the four hours of my last show I saw Bill and his "friend" Linda working in the production studio next to the FM on-air studio I was in.

There was not anything unusual about him being in the station several hours after his shift because he went into those studios nightly and created magic. He was the best production man in Columbus. (Production is the term for commercials.) Bill could do things back then with just a microphone and a tape recorder that even with today's technology it would be difficult to even come close in terms of style, delivery and imagination. He was a genius.

Aside from having the best radio voice ever, he could do hilarious impressions, make his own sound effects and was a talented musician. His guitar playing was fabulous in a sort of amusing way. His animated versions of B. B. King songs were the equivalent of Weird Al's vocal parodies.

In addition, he had this voice, actually several that the naked ear would never guess that it was him, nor would they know he was a white guy. Bill could sound blacker than any black guy I ever knew. Beemon Black would have been envious.

He could talk in these voices to make you cry with sympathy, or fall off your stool laughing. Bill could carry on conversations with himself by the magic of over dubbing that sounded like several people talking to each other.

He could sing like B.B. King well enough that if it were not for the lyrics he made up; one would not be able to tell the difference. It was in that voice, and with his blusey sounding guitar he went into the studio that night and recorded the funniest song I ever heard.

It was one of the gifts he gave me when I got off the air.

That and a pizza that had "Rastus" spelled out in pepperonis. Rastus was what Bill had nick-named me during my years at WTVN. It was my pet name around the station.

"Right on Rastus, and His Rock & Roll Record Review. It was sung and narrated by Bill to a popular song of the day called "Love Jones."

Of all of the pre-recorded funny bits Bill and I did together for his program, that last song became priceless to me. I was leaving a pretty good radio station and a pretty good friend. I left for WNCI and Bill eventually left for WBZ in Boston. At that time, WBZ was one of the biggest radio stations in the country.

And aside from a few exchanged long distance phone calls and a few letters in the years that passed we lost touch with each other. I haven't communicated with him since 1976.

The First of May

WBUK-FM-96, which in the early 1970's was located on the 16th floor of the Buckeye Federal Building at 42 East Gay Street was where I learned to appreciate what was called "Good Music" or as it is now referred to as adult standards.

Competing for older listeners back then with WBNS-FM-97 for the over 45 audience, WBUK salted it's format with some light jazz, adult Pop and vocal tracks by such artists as Ed Ames, Patti Page and The Letterman. WBNS's stock in trade was pure elevator music. When I was hired there, I was handed what amounted to as a dream job.

My taste in music at the time was more along the lines of Issac Hayes and Elton John, but I was familiar with the older music because I grew up hearing it on an old Zenith console stereo in my parent's living room.

The job was not my ultimate dream in terms of making it in radio, but it was the stepping-stone I needed for what would come later. The fact that I was hired at all was something of a miracle to those around me who had never seen me accomplish a goal previously, and who doubted any likelihood that I could get a job in radio.

I never was too good at being told that I could not do something, and allowing someone the satisfaction of seeing me give up. At no other time in my life, either before or since have I ever put so much effort into getting anything.

While the other DJ's I knew in those days were working at cool radio stations like WCOL and WNCI and playing the Rolling Stones and The Eagles, I was queuing up Erroll Garner and Lawrence Welk records on the WBUK turntables.

Not real hip for a young Hippie trying to get noticed by the Rock station programmers and managers. But none of that really mattered because I was sitting on the other side of the studio window from power house, WTVN 610-AM which was a music station at that time with enough watts to be heard all over the state of Ohio, and I knew that the FM arm of Taft Broadcasting Company (The parent company) was something like a "farm team" for the AM "Friendly Giant" as 610 was known in those days.

A lot of us ended up with double duty working on both AM and FM, and some of us moved over to WTVN from WBUK for full-time jobs. I was among the lucky ones who did.

And from the Buckeye Building I would later move up to 4900 Sinclair Road to the WNCI studios inside what was then called "The Scotts Inn Motel" to play "real" Rock & Roll. My ultimate goal was WCOL but that did not happen until ten years later, and not before I pulled stints at WRFD and WMNI.

Having worked with different music formats has allowed me to grow old with a diverse appreciation for all types of music, and because of those early days at WBUK I am quite content to listen for hours at a time to guy's like Vic Damone, Jerry Vale and Percy Faith. I have, in a musical sense, become my parents.

That first radio job at WBUK paid me the whopping sum of $2.00 per hour, a quarter more than my previous job as a janitor at the J-Mart Department Store on Demorest Road. However, I was not in it for the money as much as I was to avoid remaining a janitor for the rest of my life.

So now, when I find myself listening to Sammy Davis Junior or even Vicki Carr records I am transported back to an era of exciting transition.

I do not know if the old standards are as good as I think they sound to me now, or if just by hearing them again it makes me feel better because I remember so much about that time in my life.

Meeting and rubbing elbows with famous entertainers for the first time when they visited the Taft studios, going to press parties and actually signing a few autographs for people who thought DJs were "stars".

But more than that, I am reminded of a time when looking into the mirror and seeing gray hair, or being considered by many as over the hill was somewhere way into the future. As if it would never come. Being invincible and careless, and having more energy than any five people who I now share similarities with.

When getting laid by someone whose name did not matter.

When $2.00 an hour was enough.

The old music seems to move the clock backward as fast as it has spun forward to where I am now.

Understanding that when I was making daily phone calls to WBUK's program director Jim Lohse I was after something I wanted more than anything in the world, and that nearly four decades have passed since.

Four decades, time that was years in the future back then, and an amount of time that I won't be around to see when it goes by again. If logic didn't overwhelm me I would swear that every day that passes by now goes quicker than every minute did when I was twenty years old.

An 80 something year old friend of mine who I've known for more than 30 years, and who is a student of the Scriptures has been trying to convince me that it is actually happening. That when it seems like you blink an eye and another year has passed it is more than just seeming that way, it happened. That God is somehow rushing us to a pre ordained time, and because of what he sees as prophecy now coming true the years are now ticking away like seconds.

Stuff that is way over my head and not within reach of comprehension for me, but a theory that makes me wonder, is time really flying by now, or is it because we care about it more as we age and it just seems that way?

Something time cannot change or wear out is good music.

Candles in the Rain

As silly as this might sound, many colleges are now featuring the option of co-ed dormitories, and even any-gender restrooms. No more signs on the door designating them as for men only, or women only. The any gender restroom concept is not new, nearly everywhere, I have ever worked a night shift the women's restroom was fair game. Most men I have known would rather go there then into a men's room.

Among the reasons, women did not usually pee on toilet seats, and they always had this thing about air-fresheners and similar polite issues.

And at night when the other employees were home sleeping-it was not a problem. At WCOL the women's bathroom was just outside the on-air studio, while the men's room was down the hall, around the corner and down another hall.

You needed to look at the emergency escape plan on the wall to find it.

'COL's women's bathroom was interesting. It had its own vestibule separated by another entry door to the facilities themselves. And just inside was a bed. I will get right back to that.

When you opened the door to the men's room, you were greeted by a urinal and a sink, so if you happened to be taking a leak everyone who walked down the hall could observe. Hey, that is not as unlikely as you might think, it was a radio station, I doubt if anyone really cared on either side of the door.

Back to the bed in the women's room.

Upon entering the vestibule, one could lock the door behind them. Portable motel.

I never really understood why management would put a bed in there but the folk lore about it was that management didn't.

Wonderful stories were told about the advantages of having a bed just outside of an on-air studio at a rock station. Among them tired DJs who had slaved all day over a hot radio could relax and catch their breath before attempting to drive home. (Sure.)

Free Ride

I do not remember how many Ford Econoline vans I have owned because of my insatiable appetite for Ford products, but there were several. One of my favorites was a 1969 that I tooled around in 1979 while working at WMNI. It was the ugliest vehicle on the Great Southern Hotel's parking lot.   (Where the radio station was located.)

It had been previously owned by the Columbus Board of Education's Maintenance Division and still had all of that wording printed on the doors. My neighbors probably thought I worked as a school janitor and was blessed with a take home vehicle.

Aside from a little "surface rust" around the wheel wells and missing only one of its two front turn signal lenses, the van was in great mechanical shape and it ran great. It smoked a little and had a tendency to over-heat on hot days but it was a "runner."

My fellow radio personalities believed, and with good reason that I had fallen on hard times judging me by my "ride." WMNI did not pay a lot of money and it required a great deal of my salary to keep some of my jalopies running. The "BOE" van was as ugly inside as it was out.

It had two front seats that were in dire need of upholstery, and a tablecloth that separated the "cabin" from the back seat, which qualified only as a seat if more than one person wanted or needed to sit down while riding with me. In reality, the seat was actually a bed that I had made out of 2 X 4's and plywood. The tablecloth offered privacy from anyone peering into the side windows when the van doubled as my sleeping quarters.

I recall one afternoon when I was to accompany one of our announcers, Carl Wendelken, who was also the stations promotions director, and our program director, Steve Cantrell to some sort of press conference at what was then called the "Ohio Center" downtown, and Steve decided that I should drive "my car." He had not yet seen my van.

When we walked to the hotel parking lot, they followed me to my "car" and as I opened the rear side door to allow them to get in one of them asked what I was doing. They thought I was messing with someone else's vehicle. When I told them it was mine they looked at each other and they cracked right up.

For whatever reason they agreed to risk riding with me on the condition that I let them out a few blocks from our destination so they would not be seen riding in it.

However, I could hear the cracks and unflattering remarks exchanged between the two of them as I chauffeured them to our destination.

I don't recall if it was because I was offended by their comments, or if it was because I was simply a mean spirited sort, but for whatever my reasons, I decided to take them right up High Street to the front of the Convention Center where I parked in line with several other arrivals.

There were newer Buicks and other higher end vehicles there letting passengers out. My passengers didn't know because there were no rear windows and they could not see where we were when I stopped. They also could not get out unless I let them out because the inside door handle did not function properly.

I knew how to open it but they could have played with it for hours and never figured it out. When I did get out to open the door for them they stepped out in front of a crowd, where there were a number of other people we all recognized.

Cantrell could at times have a foul mouth.

This was one of those times. Carl on the other hand seemed to appreciate what was happening, giving himself away with his laughter. It was a beautiful thing to see. Both Steve and Carl were wearing suits to the occasion but I could not begin to remember what I was wearing. It could not have been a suit because I did not own one. The sight of these two radio "tycoons" climbing out of the back of that rusted '69 remains one of my most treasured images.

By the end of the day, I returned to the station without passengers. They had sponged a different ride back. It was not until a few years later when I traded that van in on a newer Econoline conversion van that Steve wanted me to take him somewhere.

Even though both men have since passed away, I would imagine Carl is still laughing and Steve is still cussing me. (But in his usual understanding manner.)

Steve came to know, and I think even appreciated my sometimes intentional civil disobedience.

The Anniversary Waltz

In the summer of 2008 at the 50th anniversary of the North American Broadcasting Company's venture into Columbus radio I spent a little time hanging out with an old friend who has been with the company for more than two decades. Greg Mobius and I only worked together for a few short month's back in the late 1980's, when I returned to NABCO as a part-time DJ.

Having completed several month's of training at the Franklin County Sheriff's Academy and with my boots solidly planted as a Deputy Sheriff I was offered an opportunity to "come home" for a few hours of fun and frolic each week on what was then known as WMGG-Magic-99.

Greg was one of those personalities that seemed so immersed in radio life that nothing could upset him. He was always in a good mood.

Always smiling and enthusiastic about his work.

After more than twenty years he still is. Now the company's director of promotions, and I would guess all things public affairs related, Greg has become one of those NABCO fixtures that reminds me of the pink rabbit who pounds the drums and keeps on going. Like Nick Reed the company money tracker who has been there, or at least connected in some way since the mid 1960's.

When people familiar with the often revolving door that radio is meet these guy's for the first time and hear of their tenure with the same station they might wonder how it's possible. Greg and Nick are not rare specimens within the NABCO family.

There is something about that place that makes people want to stay, and if they can survive the other trials of ratings, programming changes and personality conflicts that infect all work places from time to time, many do. Then there are those who see greener hues on the lawns on the other side of the fences. Guys like me.

Not that I am, or ever was a wander luster, I was more of the impulsive dare taker that even if I was completely happy in my environment I needed challenged, my cup needed to runneth over or I simply wanted to experience new people, places and surroundings.

Going from radio studios to police cruisers was the most glowing example of that. I still hear radio people talk about the mythical bug that injects the business into the blood streams of those who choose that forum of moneymaking, but I contend that the reasons people hang around it, even old burnouts and retired talkers like myself, is because we just like it.

As hard as I try sometimes to convince myself and other's that I don't miss being paid to make station owners and managers richer, I still enjoy writing and talking about the magicians who have made it their life's work to stay plugged into whatever it is that has kept companies like NABCO committed for decades, and for some stations just fourteen years shy of a century. In 2022 radio itself will be 100 years old.

The Heart of Rock & Roll

E very show began...
    "On the scene with a stack of shellac and his record machine. How's that grab ya jelly bean?" More than fifty years after Hoyt Locke launched rock & roll in Columbus, Ohio he remains a controversial figure, that is when stories about his sudden rise as a disk jockey phenom at WCOL are told there are multiple versions.

People seem to remember him differently, some claim to have known him well while others just embellish on what they think they know, or more likely what they heard. Take my opening statement here for example, some argue that it was not Hoyt, (aka Doctor Bop) who was the first DJ in Columbus to play rock & roll on the radio.

One spirited argument I got to that came from the late Eddie Saunders, longtime WVKO radio personality. Eddie once nearly blew a verbal gasket when I stated on the air at WCOL that Doc was the first to play R & R in Columbus, on our station in 1956, arguing that he was doing it the year before on WVKO. At that time, we had been running promos for a Doctor Bop tribute show that had been scheduled to air and he was not pleased.

It was 1984 and Edgar Locke, Hoyt's brother joined me on my nightly radio program to salute the contribution Doc made not only to WCOL, but to the overall musical culture of Columbus radio. The music, the jingles and the commercials we aired that night were all vintage late '50's and we took phone calls from listeners who shared their memories of the stations' early Rock & Roll roots, and of Doctor Bop's role in making it happen.

No one called to dispute any of what was being talked about, and in fact as the evening progressed we enjoyed an enthusiastic audience eager to legitimize Doc's historic role in changing not just one radio station, but how that affected it's competitors and an entire generation.

There was so much nostalgia being exchanged it became almost too difficult to get the listeners on the air. Everyone it seemed had a story. Secretly I was hoping Saunders would phone in and challenge us but that call never came.

In the days leading up to that program I had been listening to and dissecting an interview between Doc and former WCOL DJ Jim Davis recorded years earlier. It was similar to the show we were planning. In 1975, the station brought Doc "home" for a reunion.

An on-air show with Jim followed by a live appearance at a popular nightspot called "Studio 5." I recognized on that taped interview several former radio personnel and a few business people who participated in it; from there we went about contacting as many of them as we could.

Combining that with our own in-house research including my own notes from interviews I had with former station personnel who I had worked with at other stations. I do not believe I was ever more prepared to host a radio interview. Everywhere were testimonies that he was the first DJ to play rock music on Columbus radio. Doc himself took that credit for years.

Edgar and his wife Beatrice offered vivid details of Doc's life and shared many family photos when I visited them in their home on Buelen Road prior to my on-air interview. A WCOL engineer who had been with WCOL since 1946 believed we had thoroughly done our homework on the matter.

Back to Saunders and why I was on the receiving end of his earlier wrath. He did not like what he heard on the promos and testimonials to the guy we were giving all of this credit to. He was adamant that we were talking about the wrong guy. After reminding me of a pop music show he hosted on WVKO in 1955 called "Jumpin Jive at Five-O-Five" he remained steadfast that we were tinkering with the truth. Insisting that he was the man who first played what would become rock & roll in Columbus.

Loyalists to Eddie Saunders have for years held their ground and to their conviction that he should be forever listed as the founding father of pop music if anyone is to be so anointed. Ah... Herein lies the possibility of a truce. As Edgar pointed out, many guys were playing what was considered pop music before Hoyt became a 'COL hired hand.

However, singers like Sinatra and Duke Ellington were considered typical pop stars of the day, as were people like Doris Day, Frankie Lane and "Satch" Armstrong. "Pop stars" as Edgar called them, not Rock stars. Little Richard was a Rock star, Chuck Berry and Elvis weren't in Saunders record rack but were in the box of records that Hoyt carried into the WCOL studios to introduce to Columbus listeners.

Before the all night show was his, Hoyt was there, often as a client to record commercials for the record store he co-owned with Edgar, "The Bop Record Shop." He was making infomercials before anyone knew what they were called. The record store originally opened at 382 East Main Street in 1950 but in '56 moved to 474 East Main.

One August night that year Hoyt was at the studios to record his commercials when the DJ on the air Jim "Catman" Sherman got up and walked out leaving the station without an announcer. The station engineer asked Hoyt to take over. Soon the Locke Brothers were purchasing fifteen minute segments at the station with Hoyt as the voice, or as Edgar called him, "The Showman of the family business" Doctor Bop was created.

Fifteen minutes a night at first and soon evolving into a six-hour all night radio show. So actually in the beginning, Doctor Bop was not a paid WCOL announcer, he paid them to announce his products.

"We were merchants" Edgar said.

But apparently not very good ones because the record store was barely selling enough music to "pay the light bill" according to him. To make that happen he worked full time for the U.S. Postal Service. Not long after Hoyt began his radio career it nearly came to an end due to financial emergencies. Paying the bills at the record shop and purchasing advertising blocks to remain on the air at WCOL was taking its toll.

All of that changed when a man named George Carter who owned a City Service gas station at Garfield and Mount Vernon Avenues convinced his oil company to purchase three months of advertising on the Doctor Bop Show. That offered incentive for the station's General Manager Collie Young to make Doc its franchise announcer.

Instead of money coming out of the Locke family funds to promote what Hoyt was selling, business like City Gas, Certified Oil, the Beverly Drive-Ins, Buckeye Potato Chips and other locally owned companies were paying for it.

I mentioned other controversy surrounding Doctor Bop, then and still...then, it was about his flamboyancy, sometimes about his race and even a reputation that was often way over stated, today it is more about who he really was. How he got started, his age, and when and where he died and how old he was.

Some accounts have him dead before he was fifty years old, one suggesting that he died in his mid 40's. The fact is, Hoyt Locke, aka Doctor Bop was born March 11, 1912 in Chattanooga, Tennessee, his family moved to the south side of Columbus in the teens.

They lived for a time on Barthman Avenue where the boys were students at nearby Reeb Avenue Elementary School. As kids he and his brother roamed Parsons Avenue shining other people's shoes for pennies and hawking newspapers for a few more to take home to help support their family.

He passed away on February 24, 1976, a month shy of his 64th year.

Doctor Bop died of a heart attack in Milwaukee.

Rarely is it mentioned that after leaving WCOL in 1959 Doc went to work for his old friend Bill Mnich, a former WCOL salesman and a man who was instrumental in launching his career. Mnich had built his own radio station (WMNI) and before the end of the 1950's was competing with WCOL for the rock & roll audience.

After conflicts with 'COL management, probably over salary as most conflicts with radio managers usually are, Doc went across the dial from 1230 to the Mnich station at 920 on it for a brief period.

By 1960 the competition was not going well for the younger pop radio upstart with its rock format so Doc was on his way to WAWA in Milwaukee, Wisconsin where for the next several years he would not only star on that station but program it as well.

Much of my own version of Docs life as a Columbus radio legend comes from testimonials and insight from those who knew him. Better records of his radio career in Columbus should have been maintained by the station he helped make legendary but sadly, they were not.

Surprisingly not even tapes of Doctor Bops radio shows were left behind. Tapes do exist and I have collected a few of them, but a lot of the history of WCOL, including recordings of many of the other well known personalities who worked there over the years wasn't salvaged. Most of what remains of either recorded or printed history resides in personal archives.

But I think Doc was being honest with Davis and I'm sure Edgar still had his wits when he visited what he thought was the haunted studios at 22 South Young Street back in 1984. Haunted he said by wonderful memories left clear by the still familiar hallways and studios of where he used to hang out with his brother. "I swear he's here," Edgar would say.

Hearing people say they either knew, or hung out with Doctor Bop is not that uncommon, and if all of those who have claimed to really did, then he certainly had a lot of personal friends and colleagues. Nevertheless, safe to say that Edgar knew him better than the rest of us.

Every now and then I find myself driving through the Locke Brothers old neighborhood, mere blocks from my own and I think of the stories I have heard. And I find it fascinating that here was a black guy who grew up on those streets fighting the prejudices of the times, doing what ever it took to survive the Great Depression and used a failing little record shop to navigate his way into becoming the city's most celebrated radio personality.

On a radio station that until he showed up was owned, operated and listened to by white people. Still white owned and operated, but his influence on it changed it from an average white oriented, World War ll era Big Band music station to one catering primarily to teens and young adults of every color and making it the number one station in Columbus for the next several years.

After assuming the "Doctor" moniker in 1956 Hoyt was rarely called by his given name, at least in public. He was "Doc."

When Edgar Locke came to the WCOL studios to be on my program two and a half decades after his brother left them, he said the last time he walked out of the building he was with Hoyt, yet he described from memory before he got there the precise topography of the building at 22

South Young Street. He knew about the outside intercom that was still in use at the front door, where the button for the buzzer was that was still used to alert the DJ upstairs that a visitor was trying to get in.

He described the long hallway from the elevator on the second floor to the control room where the on air studios still were, and the two steps that went up to them. He talked of meeting people like Barry Gordy, Sam Cooke and other artists who would sometimes stop by the station, and of bumping into legendary sports announcer Jack Buck who was on staff there when 'COL aired Columbus Red Bird baseball games.

Some of those players who later went on to major league careers with the St. Louis Cardinals were often regulars around the station, many of them personal friends of his and Doc's. He shared stories of others in that building including listeners who would find ways to sneak in late at night.

Stories about radio remote broadcasts' starring Doctor Bop including one famously remembered by many of the concert on the roof of Dan's Drive-In on South High Street in 1958.

Conway Twitty was an unknown pop singer at the time and he had a song coming out called "Only Make Believe. Because of the large crowd that showed up it was decided to put him on the roof. The whole event created a massive traffic jam on Route 23 from the southern tip of Franklin County to nearly its northern border.

There were stories about parties, some of them underground, the Mt. Vernon Avenue entertainment strip, an area known for its many nightclubs and other musical venues and how Doc could go into any of them and never have to spend a dime.

A world that was lit by neon and serenaded by Rhythm and Blues.

As close as anyone ever came to telling in print the total story of Doctor Bop was my late, long time friend and two-time boss, Phil Sheridan (WNCI-WRMZ). Phil was not only a master at radio station management and innovative ideas, he was an accomplished writer.

A regular columnist for various publications, and the author of several books. Including one he was working on that might have been the most compelling of all local broadcasting history books; it was to be called "Radio Daze." That book never came to print and we lost Phil a few years ago.

So unless his notes are shared and the torch is passed to another writer passionate about radio and its history we may never find out all that he was working on or how much he knew about WCOL's and Doctor Bops history.

But in the last conversation I had with Phil he talked about being in contact with surviving members of the Locke family who could have shared valuable information and possibly some rare photographs, but according to him, to put it politely, he was unable to make them understand that no one would be willing to offer great deals of money for their cooperation.

I sensed the family stories were for sale, but as Phil would often say, a book of mostly local interest does not usually garner great wealth. So that leaves us at least for now where we are, speculation entwined with facts, making for interesting debates.

Doctor Bop

Midnight Man

When I joined the Obetz Police Department in September, 1995, I knew that I had found a home away from home. I was surrounded by a group of pretty good officer's who had made the task of protecting the Village of Obetz an art more than a science.

Each officer was as different from the others as they were diverse in their backgrounds. Moreover, the guy who made it all work was our Chief, Francis "Bo" Smith. Chief Smith had formed his legacy as a retired Deputy Chief from the Columbus Division of Police. Not ready to call it a day after retiring more than 30 years from Columbus, Bo went on to serve another eleven years as our Chief. Just being around him made all of us better.

One particular officer in our midst was Emmett Ferrin. By far the most interesting cop I have ever known. Ferrin, also a former Columbus officer was sometimes the calm before the storm. Often he was the reason for the storm but his attitude toward police work was probably the best approach ever devised. That is, do your job, do not get anyone hurt and learn to do it all with a smile.

Cops like getting free stuff, especially free coffee and snacks. Emmett had honed his skills at getting free stuff so well that those he served looked forward to serving him. I remember my first few days with the department I was miffed at seeing him opening packages of hot-dogs and putting them on the grill at our favorite watering hole, Sunoco.

And as he waited for them to cook, he would slip behind the counter and spell the clerk. There stood Emmett, in uniform, ringing up customers.

When I say in uniform he wore only what was necessary to identify himself as a police officer. Nothing fancy on his shirt, no medals, no insignias, not even a name tag. Just a badge. In those days he didn't even wear a gun belt. He carried his firearm in his pocket. I thought it was strange, but Emmett thought the rest of us were. He would look at my attire and ask if I really needed all of that.

He would make fun of my gun belt that carried pepper spray, handcuffs, ammo magazines, a pocketknife, a nightstick and a holster for my gun, and he would ask, "Are you going to use all of that stuff tonight?" Emmett had another strange idea about having more than one officer on the streets at one time. He would say things like "One riot, one cop."

Those times when I would call him to back me up he would show up and ask, "Now what did you get yourself into?" He was not big on looking for ways to stay busy. On the contrary. Emmett would rather avoid looking for trouble. However, when trouble found him he had a knack for solving it as quickly and as simply as possible.

He did not spend a lot of time looking to write tickets, but if someone was misbehaving behind the wheel, Emmett was quick to pull them over and tell them to knock it off. His way of enforcing laws could actually be comical. He was a master at stern warnings. Emmett did his job well and he did so without forcing hefty fines on violators. He enjoyed making me feel guilty every time I wrote someone a ticket by saying things like "You just took food off that guys table, or because of you, he might not be able to pay his rent or buy his kid shoes."

Emmett Ferrin retired long before I was promoted to the position of Chief of Police. In fact, he did not live to see it. He passed away following a massive heart attack shortly after his retirement. He was only in his mid 50's.

It is hard to lose friends like Emmett Ferrin. It is also a shame that the village of Obetz lost a police officer like him. I am sure he took whatever mold he was crafted from with him. Every time I drive through

Obetz and see a young cop posing in all of his glory next to a traffic violator I have to chuckle and imagine the fun Emmett would have had dressing this officer down. As I said, he had a way of reminding us to stop being so impressed with being a cop.

Nightshift

After Sgt. Ferrin moved on to another shift, Sergeant Jim Triplett took over the responsibilities for "C-Company" or, third shift patrol. This was good news for us because "Trip" as we called him behind his back was all of that and more. Sometimes he really was a trip.

Armed with a yellow highlighter Sgt. Triplett would "highlight" every mistake he could find on any report taken by any officer.

Misspelled words, missing commas, anything right down to borderline nit picking.

Because of this, I would spend more time checking, double-checking and sometime triple checking anything I wrote. I did this for the satisfaction of "beating" the sergeants yellow highlighter. I seldom did because he could always find something. There were times I thought he would pencil in mistakes, highlight them and blame me.

Nevertheless, the reality of it all was just a friendly competition. I never worked for better sergeants than Ferrin and Triplett. My eventual promotion to that rank would not have happened without these guys. Because above all else they were, they were good cops and good mentors.

Unlike Sgt. Ferrin before him, Sgt. Triplett went out of his way to keep me busy. Ferrin, who would ask "Are you going to do this a lot?"

every time I made a traffic stop didn't want us to get too busy on the job. By contrast, Sgt. Triplett would ask, "Are you ever going to do any work?"

He went as far as to geode me into a performance competition. That is, if he saw me preparing to make a traffic stop he would somehow slide in front of me and make the stop himself. At the end of the day, he would turn in more citations and more offense reports than the rest of us whom he supervised. However, that was okay, it kept him happy. Moreover, it kept the rest of us a little sharper than we would have been without him.

Sgt. Triplett, like me was an animal lover. He even carried dog-treats in the cruiser with him that he would pass out to roaming K-9's or to give to family pets when he entered homes to take reports or investigate complaints. On one occasion, he came across a pup running loose on a country road and called me for "back-up" to catch it and get it safely off the road and to someone who could care for it.

There we were, about two in the morning, crawling on the ground and baby talking to this dog to coax it out from under the sergeant's cruiser. We did get it and then went about our other responsibilities. I remember thinking that night that I worked for a pretty good guy.

As time went on I inherited his supervisory position and he moved up to the rank of captain. After he retired from the department, he ran successfully for a seat on the Obetz City Council. He is presently serving his second term there.

I am no longer a member of the Obetz family, but because of the people I worked with for ten pretty good years I will always feel like a distant cousin. Maybe in some cases a step-brother.

Lady in Red

For all of its life, from when it was new to the "oldie" it is now, I have never cared for the song "Lady in Red." Anytime it would come on the radio I would aim the old index like a missile at the channel changer and look for something better to hear.

Not that the song was horrible, but because like other song's, I remember where I was and what I was doing when I first heard it, or at least when I first noticed it, or when it had the greatest impact on my emotions.

January, 1987.

I was sent to an address on Linworth Road to hook up with Franklin County homicide detectives who were on their way to investigate what was first believed to be a double murder. By the time I got there, a perimeter had already been established around the residence with the familiar yellow "Sheriff's Line Do Not Cross" tape and several reporters who had heard the call go out on their scanners were already gathering.

My job as always was to assemble them and explain the routine, "I'll tell you something when I know something" and to remind them to observe the tape. This morning would be easier for them to do that because it was cold and blustery and most were anxious to return to their vehicles because I had promised that it was going to be a long day.

Inside the upscale home was a crime scene that investigators would soon determine to be a murder-suicide, not a double murder. When I went in to discuss with them how much information they would be willing to release I could tell I was in the home of a music man, probably someone involved with rock & roll, probably an artist and by the decor probably a successful one.

At least two shots both fired at close range, a shotgun on the floor and two victims not recognizable on opposite sides of the room.

One on his back, the other slumped in a recliner. When I exited the house and walked back to my car a radio reporter I knew well spotted me and tapped on my window wanting to know what I knew, when I told him I would need a few minutes to gather my notes he asked if I knew who lived there. I told him that we were not prepared to say, but I would tell him as soon as I could.

He asked if "Bobby Gene" was one of the victims, as if he knew him personally. I told him I could not confirm anything until I was sure that the next of kin of both had been properly notified. When he asked if "Linda Sue" was a victim I knew that he knew who was lying inside. But I still could not confirm it. I watched him get into his car and drive around the corner and I began writing a crude release that I would soon read to the others.

My police radio was on but was drowned out by the AM radio when WTVN's news began with "breaking news." It was the reporter who had just minutes earlier sat next to me in my car announcing that Bobby Gene McNelley, formerly of the popular Country-Rock band, "McGuffey Lane" was believed to have been shot and that investigators on the scene weren't yet confirming, but believed the second victim to be the musicians girlfriend, Linda Sue Green. I had been betrayed.

Times like this one were among the reasons I learned to sometimes distrust even my closest friends in the media. Sickened and worried that WTVN's listeners may have heard the news before the victim's families I changed the channel on the radio.

The song "Lady in Red" was playing on WNCI. Hoping that the detectives had been able to beat WTVN with the news to family and loved one's of the victims I went back inside to ask.

I was told that next of kin had been notified and that I had once again dodged Sheriff Earl Smith's foot up my ass. As it were, the Sheriff had heard the news on the radio when I did and had called the same detective to ask the same question I needed an answer to.

I don't know when I next heard the song "Lady In Red" but I know that when I did it reminded me of a morning on the job that I wanted to forget, and I knew that I didn't want to hear it.

Ever again.

Who Let The Dogs Out?

Not all of my war stories are horror stories from my post broadcasting life.

Corporal Dennis Verbance, then of the Sheriff's community relations office was one of those cops who I always thought missed his calling in life. Shortly after I joined the department Denny and I were thrown together in an office not because we were expected to work together as much as lack of office space.

Working one desk away from anyone and the odds are very good that two people can be expected to form a bond. Not that our jobs had anything to do with each other, mine in media relations and Denny a school resource officer before that position had a title.

Much of his work was in the schools and eventually he would become the county's first D.A.R.E. Officer and along the way come up with creative things that he would involve me.

Back to thinking that he may have missed his calling.

It was not difficult working with or hanging around with this guy because he was so likeable; it was however hard to be around him all day every day without breaking up constantly, because he was a gifted comedian without trying to be one.

Had he not chosen law enforcement Denny could have made a good living in the field I had left, a perfect fit for any morning zoo like radio show because of his attitude and unique way of expressing his views. Among the projects I would find myself working with him was his "McGruff the Crime Dog" venture.

After talking our Chief Deputy into finding the funding to purchase the "McG" costume, $600.00 at the time and at the time a ton of money, Denny talked me into wearing it at a few engagements that he arranged.

He was a smoothie, he even talked local car dealer Fred Ricart into loaning us his $200,000.00-plus Lamborghini Countache, and allowing us to dress it up with Sheriff's stickers and Red and Blue flashing lights to use in special drunk driving productions we did at local high schools.

As for the dog saga, he was the real McGruff, but some of his programs required him to be the dog's handler and the speaker of safety issues as "Deputy Denny" as the kids knew him. I will go to my grave believing that anytime he asked me to climb into the suit he knew it was going to be sweltering hot that day.

One could lose a few pounds a day wearing that heavy head of fur, furry dog paws and a heavy trench coat every day, especially days in July and August as I did more times than Denny needed me to do it. I will also die someday still believing that he had me wear that thing on day's he had nothing planned.

I think he asked me to wear it to places he had to be anyway whether or not it had anything to do with pep talks about crime prevention because when we arrived at some destinations it was obvious they weren't expecting McGruff and leaving me stuck in a hot suit with nothing to do but follow him around.

Like I said, he was a comedian. The entire program was his; I was just a fill in on hot days. Even though he and I both had take home vehicles we often found ourselves in route to various locations in the same car and sometimes we would find our days spent doing very un-police type work.

One particular day we stopped at a motel on West Broad Street for one reason or another and got hung up there all day trying to arrange for food, lodging and transportation for a family who had been traveling and were stranded. There old car had broken down and they were penniless.

And like so many other times that he was the one who got us into something he asked me, "What the Hell did you get me into?" Not that my own heart wasn't as big as his in cases like this one but it was his idea to involve us and I probably cussed him for complicating our day. He was a good cop and for a number of years a good friend.

In the years after I left the Sheriff's office and joined the Obetz Police Department he and I remained friends and I was always glad to see him in my new jurisdiction anytime he found his way south. And each time we crossed paths I was still laughing as we went our separate ways.

If I happen to outlive him, or if I'm still around if and when he ever decides to retire and everyone else we ever knew dies before us, I could write episodes that would be way more fun than this little bit of trivia. Denny taught me so much about not only being a cop, but how to keep a job like that from taking over your sanity.

When we were not busy McGruffing, or giving safety lectures to high school kids we actually did a little police work together. We did a lot of that now that I think about it. Special duty jobs mostly, but it's where I learned the fine art of running radar and writing speeding tickets and how to make people who were being arrested see the bright side of things. Denny made even them crack up.

All the Girls I've Loved Before

Working around Sheriff's detectives who investigate prostitutes and the men who pay them was never a part of my job that I cared much about.

In the early day's as Sheriff Earl Smith's Public Information Officer I was sent along on what seemed a relentless assault on sex and drug crimes, often the investigation of one led to the other.

Smith was making a name for himself for having no mercy on adult bookstores, massage parlors, strip clubs and other bastions of sex for sale or trade. It seemed we were hitting one of them every other night in the late 1980's and closing them down as "public nuisances."

I never really understood that reasoning, even though it was never in question that along with dirty books and blow jobs for sale, and girls and sometimes boys for rent, I could put up a good argument that if the public wasn't into any of it they didn't have to go into these places. The legal violations were rampant of course and Smith's morality issues were well taken, but I always' thought it was a waste of taxpayers money and ill used manpower.

The bookstores were all crab traps in that they were filthy, littered with soaked-in-semen tissues on the floors and every variation of condom and French tickler one could imagine, not to mention the smell of dirty sex everywhere. Smith argued that aside from the illicit sex and drug trade that flourished in these dumps they presented a health hazard.

He reasoned that when men would lock themselves into the private viewing booths where they could watch silent porn, they would be sitting on a seat soiled by other men's dried (hopefully) semen.

Moreover, for those daring enough to insert their penis into the holes of the walls that separated each booth the dangers could be devastating. Hoping maybe for an amorous feeling "neighbor" on the other side an idiot like that might find a Zippo or a pair of scissors waiting. Alternatively, someone with a dirty mouth or a crushing death grip.

Who takes such chances? So after the sin dens we went. Arresting prostitutes and Johns and collecting evidence (yuck) and hanging signs when we left that read "Closed by order of the Sheriff."

I guess I was fortunate to have had all of this as part of my law enforcement education because it gave me appreciation for the guys and dolls who investigate these cases. And like my other documentations of my past, I have my favorite war stories.

My favorite whore story was told by an investigator who I knew when we were teenagers working in downtown Columbus at Bonanza Steak House. I guess it was more of that fate stuff that he and I would end up working at the same place as adults, me a clean cut media relations officer and he a longhaired bearded, scruffy undercover cop.

I will call him Mike, actually that is his name so why not. After raiding and shutting down the "Gentleman's Bookstore" that sat on High Street about a block north of Main Street one night, Mike and I were standing outside smoking a cigarette and he was telling me about working undercover there to gather evidence and reasons to execute a search warrant.

I must have looked shameless when I busted out laughing when he told in detail how while walking through the narrow isles of the private viewing section he walked up on one guy with his pants down to his socks, bent over and a bigger, more burly man riding him from behind and slinging him from side to side like a blow up doll.

Violently, like a sex starved addict who had been deprived for way too long.

The mental visual of that was not as funny as the way Mike's face looked while talking about it. He said the "dude taking it from behind" had a cigarette dangling from his lip and seemed to be smiling while the bigger man was huffing and puffing and making guttural sounds. "It was the scariest thing I ever saw" Mike said.

"Especially when the big guy winked at me."

I am sorry, that was funny no matter how I frame it in my own theatre. Here was a seasoned, rather rough around the edges undercover cop who had been around the department for years openly saying that seeing two men in a dark corner having weird sex scared him.

Mike probably hand cuffed some of the most dangerous thugs and hoods in the county throughout his career and this raised his heartbeat? I could not get that exchange out of my head when I was briefing the reporters with television cameras, some of whom rode along with us on several missions. Nearly impossible to talk about the seriousness of why we were shutting down yet another business when I had to keep asking if I could have a moment.

The reporters from channels 4 and 10 knew I was not having my shiniest night and luckily, they paused their feeds a few times so I could stop laughing and gather my thoughts.

Channel 6 on the other hand hated us; they really hated the Sheriff and me by association I think. They recorded and later aired parts of my briefing, including when I laughed as I tried to explain the nuisance factor of these dirty little places.

Once these *"criminals"* were rounded up and taken to the jail some of the dirtier and more infected ones had to be checked by the jail's medical staff. Photos that I was privy to of some of the women's infested genitalia were as gruesome as anything I ever looked at and I saw some bad things at different crime scenes.

A head with holes made by bullets or limbs torn off in vehicle crashes were not as disgusting as boils as big as grapefruits between a woman's legs. Puss filled and bleeding lesions, multi colored secretions leaking from various sores and body orifices and rashes up down their thighs. This was the stuff other people paid to have sex with?

One had to assume they did business in the dark because if anyone saw what they were pressing up against or into it would be inconceivable that they would rent the space in the first place.

Some of these people were poster kids for every SDS imaginable.

I often wondered how anyone could get so horny to not only willingly have sex with these people, but pay for it.

Sheriff Smith was right, some idiot gets naked and snuggles up to that and then goes home and sits on the same furniture his wife and kids do, baths in the same bath tub, sits on the same commode and God forbid, has sex with the mother of his children. "Honey, have you ever seen a rash like this?" And, "Why is that thing so swollen?"

Being a self described moderate conservative with liberal leanings I would be among the last to suggest policing the sexual boundaries of where adults are willing to hang out, and never would I sign onto anything that dictates what grown-ups read, or what kind of pictures they look at.

However, we do shake hands with many people as we navigate through our daily routines and we do grab doorknobs, railings and other things that might leave tiny microcosms on our fingers. We also sometimes eat in places where others prepare our food and handle the silverware we put into our mouths and we pay through the nose for the health issues some people bring onto themselves, especially those who might be uninsured and *often* in need of medical attention.

And, because so many people who live in the sex trade are addicted to other illicit and expensive habits, the other crimes they may commit to stay in business can be not only costly but also dangerous to everyone else. Sheriff Smith was right, spouses and significant others do place others besides themselves in jeopardy when they take that walk on the wild side.

All of that said, I still think that we spent entirely too much money and energy trying to rid the county of naughty behavior.

More than twenty years after our still talked about sweeps and round-ups, Franklin County still has numerous massage parlors, strip clubs and adult bookstores and more whores on more corners than ever before.

In twenty years from now, their sons and daughters will be out there offering a little for a lot. The trade will always flourish.

Duke of Earl

For all of the reasons some did not like Earl Smith, Franklin County Sheriff 1985-1993, I did. Mean if he needed to be, outspoken always and maybe the best Sheriff in Franklin County history.

Earl might argue that Stacy Hall Sr. was the best ever, I know he respected him and even voiced that sentiment to me. I think he thought of his mentor as I did of mine. All I know of Stacy is what has been written in local history books and what has been spoken by some who either worked for him, or wrestled him.

In his better days he was a feared grappler in local wrestling arenas. Earl called him, "the toughest cop I ever knew." Other deputies who worked for him echoed those sentiments. Smith was something like that to me, but in a different way.

I appreciate men like him who came from the era when it was okay to sass the world around them if they thought the world around them was out of line.

Cussing out loud, if it helped to enhance his thoughts, or blowing smoke into the face of anyone daring to tell him to douse his cigarette, or for that matter anyone daring to tell him to do anything.

He was the Sheriff and that office afforded awesome powers.

Chief law enforcement officer of the entire county, more authority than any Mayor inside *his* county, any Chief of Police or anyone in the

State Highway Patrol. The "High Sheriff." And this one happened to be tough; if a person was an ass, or if he just thought they were he would call them an ass hole.

Not when they couldn't hear him, he preferred they knew.

He would do that with broadcast microphones in his face or television cameras aimed at him, or if talking to a journalist or the suspected ass himself, especially if the journalist was an ass, or one that wrote unflattering remarks about him or his office.

Moreover, Earl did not discriminate; it did not matter if they were other cops, political opponent's judges or the President of the local chapter of the Fraternal Order of Police. An ass needed to be labeled properly, and out loud.

I remember a certain female reporter saying to me that Earl was the most vulgar man she ever met because he told her in a rather frank manner to do something of a sexual nature to herself. She claimed that was the most insulting thing anyone ever said to her.

I enjoyed sharing media morsels like that with the Sheriff and when I told him what the reporter said about him he stated, "She must have lived a charmed life if that really was the most insulting thing anyone ever said to her."

Or she's a liar." *Earl O. Smith, circa 1986*

As I said, I liked getting him fired up and I always' knew that sort of thing would push that button.

As for the reporter, I tried to soften the insult by reminding her that the Sheriff had also told a couple of County Commissioners to similarly "F" themselves that very same day. Earl had pet names for two of the three sitting commissioners.

"Fritz and Tits."

My favorite "Earl -vs- Everyone" moment was when another female reporter demanded that she be given a tour of the Franklin County Jail, even though the Sheriff hated her gut's and told me not to let her in.

After selling the idea to him that it might be good public relations to let television viewers see what deputies have to deal with every day he softened by telling me to take her on the floor that housed what he called "our freaks."

A floor that housed men who might do such things as strip naked, masturbate and throw product at anyone walking by through the bars, or defecate into their palms and sling that at them.

Spitters, and verbal assailants who might spit in your face if their aim was good, and might promise to do awful things to you and your mother at the same time.

Some of those men liked to tell you things about your mother, your wife and even your kids. That was where the Sheriff wanted this reporter.

"Take her up there, let her see what we deal with, let her get a taste (I think he meant that literally) of the people she thinks we should be treating better." She had previously nagged the Sheriff about jail procedures after receiving a letter from an inmate who had complained about the food, the amount of time allowed for exercise and over-crowding in the jail.

And, although the food in there was lousy and playtime might have been limited, most of his anguishes could have been explained by that third complaint.

So her journey began and ended on that floor of the downtown facility. When I told the sheriff that during her tour an inmate threw a cup of urine into her face, he just nodded and said, "Good for him." He was smiling. I had made his day.

Some days could be difficult though, made more so by those standing in long lines to make it tough on everyone by trying to destroy him and his administration.

Sometimes it was me they were after. He may have had as many enemies as he had admirers, but like he was proud to say and say often, he was not trying to win a popularity contest. He said that but I knew different.

I think what he really meant was that he enjoyed the notoriety, good, bad or indifferent but he wanted respect. And, of those who wished him gone, for some it may not have been because they disliked Earl, but because of someone in his office.

Maybe a Chief Deputy that was disliked or other high-ranking officers who had their own circles of enemies and some who perhaps were engaging in their own power struggles.

Still, Earl Smith had a knack for making enemies, and sometimes it was not even about a policy or a decision, sometimes it was just because of his attitude. There were few opportunities for anyone to win an argument with him. Maybe he was a lawman way ahead of his time.

His actions and attitudes would have been, and probably were revered during the Stacy Hall era and in the years that preceded.

There was a time when county sheriffs carried bigger sticks than most do now, and were more willing to use the stick with less concern for public opinion. He may have lacked the social graces and the political savvy of others who have occupied that office, but what he had will be missed by those were loyal to him. I miss him.

That is because Earl Smith and I had more in common than just growing up on the Southside and being South High School alumni, he and I *got* it. I understood him and I think I was able to make him understand me.

The sheriff's office, although probably the most political of all elective offices should be more about law enforcement and keeping the public safe than it should ever be about politics. Few departments in Ohio operate that way now.

Few sheriffs are willing to do all that they know or think is right, regardless of political appearance or for fear of how they might be perceived, especially by the media. Earl Smith may have been the last Sheriff who did not care. And I got that.

Friends

Danny James Davis (DJ) was the first *best* friend I had on the block I still live on, and more than fifty years after I first met him similar friendships have come, gone, come back again and went away again.

DJ was a freckled faced kid about my age at the time (6) and I thought I would know him the rest of my life. The friendship lasted almost until we were teenagers, a lifetime then. Although his parents and mine only knew each other as neighbors, they treated us as if we were theirs.

Always looking out for us, worrying about us and even taking us along on each other's family outings once in awhile. My next best friend on the block was Shane Sheaf. Somewhere in the middle of about seven kids in the Sheaf family, Shane and I were inseparable in the early 1960's.

That is unless one of us decided for a day that DJ was our best friend. (My best skirmishes to date were with these guys.) And like DJ, I thought Shane and I would never *not* know each other. That too lasted almost until we were teenagers. And like the Davis family, the Sheafs moved away before we were in high school and by then all of us were beginning to forget each other and start making new friends.

After more than three decades of not knowing one another, Shane and I bumped into each other one day, and for the past few years we've tried to stay in touch through emails and occasionally we try to get together to enjoy each others company and reminisce about who we were and who we've become.

And by the fifth grade, I had a new best friend, Delmas Jeffries. "Sonny" as I knew him would remain a dear friend until we were both in our mid forties, and then around 1997 he seemingly dropped off the face of the earth.

I have no idea where he is now or how to find him or even *why* he and I no longer know each other. But like another former *best friend*, Danny Sauer who I wrote about in an earlier chapter, I'm guessing that Sonny and I just ran out of things to talk about, or maybe as the years skipped by we simply found that we no longer had much in common.

Then, like now, I guess it is safe to say I could count my friends on one hand. In addition, to paraphrase a line in the 1986 movie, *"Stand By Me"* narrated by Richard Dreyfuss, we never have friends like the ones we had when we were twelve years old. However, through the years I have claimed a few more *best friends* during my journeys through broadcasting and law enforcement.

And although I no longer communicate regularly with *any* of them, I still consider some of them as important as any I claimed through childhood. There are some radio and television personalities out there who I owe much to for helping me find my communication bearings and for helping me hone my bullshitting skills, and there are *many* cops who I owe much more than that.

A few who helped me see that we live in a world sometimes surrounded by bullshit, and a few more that saved my ass enough times that I am still around and able to pen whatever all of this is.

All of that said, I no longer have a best friend.

I *know* many people and it may be safe to say that I have *some* friends, but what *is* sure is that I can still count the best of them on just the one hand. And most of them I think will agree.

Paperback Writer

I have been writing this book for a number of years, not knowing that it would someday be a book. What I have shared is notes I have kept both written and archived in memory. E. Karl taught me years ago to document what may someday be important. To keep diaries of things we do not want to forget.

Because if we just do things and forget it, what was the point? Just passing through or killing time until we die? I mentioned earlier that this is a book that describes what I consider some personal triumphs and some personal failures. Some may not understand my candor, or the reasons why I would share all that I have.

Nevertheless, as I reflect on what I think was an interesting life; I come to the conclusion that if I do not share as much as I can than what *was* the point. Not everyone gets to experience what I have. I have pulled back a few curtains and offered a behind the scenes glimpse into things that have made me smile, frustrated me, encouraged me and challenged me.

Moreover, along the way a few reasons why. Besides, everything in this book is out there whether I write it or not.

Dedicated to my family:

Mary, Todd, Kevin, Ricky, Joey, Kelly, Bob, Pat and Susie.

And to Dee Jaye

Rick Minerd